Compassion

for

All

Creatures

Compassion for All Creatures

An Inspirational Guide for Healing the Ostrich Syndrome

JANICE GRAY KOLB

Blue Dolphin Publishing
1997

Published by Blue Dolphin Publishing, Inc.
P.O. Box 8, Nevada City, CA 95959
Orders: 1-800-643-0765
Internet: http://www.bluedolphinpublishing.com
ISBN: 1-57733-008-0

Library of Congress Cataloging-in-Publication Data

Kolb, Janice G.
    Compassion for all creatures : an inspirational guide for healing the
ostrich syndrome / Janice Gray Kolb.
        p. cm.
    Includes bibliographical references.
    ISBN 1-57733-008-0
    1. Animals—Religious aspects—Christianity.   2. Animal welfare—
Religious aspects—Christianity.   I. Title.
BT746.K63   1997
241'.693—dc21   97-11553
                                                                                    CIP

All illustrations and photographs are by the author with the exception of:
First photograph of Rochester Harry Kolb by Francis J. Egan
Two Hudson photographs (pg. 214) and Sweetpea (pg. 145)
    by June L. Kolb Hudson
Three Clancy photographs (pp. 166, 172) by Dennis, Patti, and Terry Clancy
Photograph of author with Rochester by Bob Kolb
Cover design: Lito Castro

A portion of any profits realized by sales of this book will be used in
overcoming the ostrich syndrome.

Printed in Canada by Best Manufacturing

9   8   7   6   5   4   3   2   1

This Book
is
Dedicated

to
Bob

and
Rochester

and
in the
luxury of remembrance
of
thirteen precious friends who entered
Heaven
during the writing and publication of this book:

Francis J. McGeary
Robert E. Gottlieb, Jr.
Edward J. Wall, Jr.
Rev. Msgr. William H. Flatley
Barry R. Greene
John Jennings
Mary L. Coakley
My uncle — George Gray
Joseph F. Clancy
Sr. Mary Nolasco O'Hara, SSJ

and
beloved family companions

Molly Hudson and Stuffy Drakely (canine)
Sweet Pea Hudson (feline)

Rochester Harry Kolb

Table of Contents

Foreword

FOLKLORE HAS TOLD US that when the ostrich is in trouble or in a situation where he doesn't want to be aware of reality, he buries his head in the sand—thus blocking out anything in his life that may be disturbing or undesirable. The fact that this is not the actual way the ostrich responds to dangerous reality does not matter for our purposes. The meaning of this title and the goal of this book are:

- to consider the station of animals and their relationship to us in a world that we share;
- to reconsider our responsibilities to them, both physical and moral;
- to be able to say to ourselves and to each other, "Stop sticking your head in the sand, my friend, so you won't be forced to observe reality";
- to see and understand the things that would make any normal, clear-thinking man or woman want to respond to the horror being perpetrated on the animals of this world; and
- to get off our comfortable posteriors and DO SOMETHING.

Consider whether you have been dulled and conditioned by the habits, platitudes, and opinions that society has nurtured in you. Perhaps you have become so passive that you respond only to the buttons pushed by those of our society who mold our thought. If you can be constantly exposed to moral injustice and downright cruelty and really not even see it—*then this book is for you*. At last, after reading this book, you'll be able to pull your head out of the sand, wipe the grit out of your eyes, and look around and really see. Perhaps then you'll join society's ever-increasing group of thinking and compassionate people who want to end this tyranny and escape from "the ostrich syndrome."

When we humans wish to block from our senses the reality of unpleasantnesses that surrounds us, we ignore these situations, pretending they don't exist—much the same as the ostrich. We stifle and degrade our sense of compassion to the point where we are not unlike the ostrich. He has wings which enable him to run in a stable way—but never to ascend.

One evening, the author and I were talking about some new outrage of cruelty that had been visited upon a defenseless creature, when I commented to her that many people, hearing the same report that we had just heard, would respond with complete apathy. They would stick their heads in the sand like the mythical ostrich and wait until the horror departed. I said that they were suffering from "the ostrich syndrome." *"That's it!"* Jan said. *"That's what I'm going to call the new book I'm writing about animals. It expresses how I feel when otherwise good and moral religious people often fail to consider or exhibit even basic compassion for animals and their rights."*

So we have dubbed this condition, which occurs when humans ignore the outrageous sufferings of animals, "the ostrich syndrome." It is a unique set of conditions that compound to create a situation where we humans can comfortably ignore the reality of the horrors that we are immersed in. It exists for each of us, as we are an integral part of this moral cesspool, by consent or by comfortably ignoring the facts, in order to protect our own comfort, while blindly permitting the horror to surround us. It is allowed to prosper when we as individuals stand by and permit our social culture to go along, smiling at each other, convinced that we as a group and as individuals are "nice guys."

Let's take a step back and try to look at ourselves and our culture from a position of disembodiment. We can then be more analytic about the situation and see what we have become. All it takes for this evil to persist and prosper is for "nice guys" like us to laughingly put our heads in the sand and pretend that everything is not only proper but "OK."

In an inaugural address, President Franklin Delano Roosevelt said, "We must live as men—not as ostriches." Although he was commenting on our national concerns about isolationism and a world that was becoming increasingly complex, we might use the same phrase when thinking about animals. When we face the issue squarely, giving it the attention it deserves, we will be taking a giant step toward opening our minds and hearts to the profound world of consciousness that surrounds us all.

—Robert A. Kolb Jr.

✿

Dear Father, hear and bless
Thy beasts and singing birds,
And guard with tenderness
Small things that have no words.

—Anonymous

✿

I am the voice of the voiceless;
Through me the dumb will speak.
'Til the deaf world's ear be made to hear
The wrongs of the wordless weak.

And I am my brother's keeper,
And I will fight his fight;
And speak the word for beast and bird
'Til the world shall set things right.

—Ella Wheeler Wilcox
1850-1919

✿

Unseen they suffer
Unheard they cry—

✿

In the glance of the speechless animal there is a discourse
that only the soul of the wise can really understand.

—an Indian Poet
(from *The Treasury of Kahlil Gibran*)

We need another and a wiser and perhaps a more mystical concept of animals. We patronize them for their incompleteness, for their tragic fate of having taken form so far below ourselves. And therein we err, and greatly err. For the animal shall not be measured by man. In a world older and more complete than ours they move, finished and complete, gifted with extensions of the senses we have lost or never attained, living by voices we shall never hear. They are not brethren, they are not underlings, they are other nations, caught with ourselves in the net of life and time, fellow prisoners of the splendour and travail of the earth.

—Henry Beston
(from his book, *The Outermost House*, the enduring classic of a solitary year of life in a small cottage on the Great Beach of Cape Cod)

Acknowledgments

All glory to my Christ and
I wish to thank my Guardian Angel
and special angels who are ever present.

I wish to thank St. Francis of Assisi
and
St. Martin de Porres
for their great love and protection of all God's creatures while they were here on earth and for their intercession on their behalf, which continues in Heaven. A plaque and statue of them in my writing room are symbolic of this intercession and were a presence to me during the writing of this book.

🐾 I wish to express my extreme appreciation to Paul M. Clemens, publisher of Blue Dolphin Publishing, for believing in this book and to all of his capable staff who helped in so many ways.

🐾 I wish to thank Rochester for his constant love, presence, inspiration, and devotion throughout our life together. Because of him this book was written.

🐾 I wish to thank my husband Bob for his love and support and our life together in New Hampshire that makes it possible to write. I am grateful, too, for the time he gave in endless hours typing this manuscript.

🐾 I am grateful to my parents, Ellis and Violet Gray, for their love and for having a little cat in our home before I was born and for allowing me the wonderful experience of continually living with cats for twenty-one years. I am grateful also for the shorter period during which we had a dog join our family.

❧ I wish to thank my daughter Janna for her continuing encouragement of my writing, for her help and interest in this book in numerous ways, and for "being there" to bring Rochester into my life.

❧ A special thank you to my son George for his prayers and support of my writing—and for being responsible for first giving our family the joy of sharing our home with animals—and who now shares his home with his papillon dog, Tess.

❧ A special thank you to Jessica, my daughter, who brought Katie into our hearts and home—and for the many special joys and experiences we three shared together, and for your love and prayers, Jessica.

❧ With love I mention gratefully my daughters June, Laurel, and Barbara, who are always there for me with their love and encouragement. Thank you, Laurel, for reading my manuscript. A special thank you to Francis for his love, his interest, our talks, and his computer help—and to my other sons(in-law) and daughter(in-law), Rob, Bob, Michael, Bill, and Valerie, for their love.

❧ I wish especially to thank my dear friend Ruth Depman for her constant interest in and prayers for this book—and for her continually giving me articles pertaining to animals and beautiful journals in which to record my thoughts—and for her encouraging letters.

❧ A thank you also to my good and long-time friend, Rev. Ginny Leopold, for prayers, interest, and for her always available HOT-LINE of help regarding my animal concerns (or any concern)—and for making me laugh.

❧ To dearest Rose-Beth Woolley Pierson, in gratitude for her love and constancy in so many ways—and for our loving exchanges about Nora, Buck, Willy, and Rochester. We shall remember Nora, who passed away July, 1996, forevermore.

❧ My gratitude to my special friend Dan Deane for his prayers and "Musings" and interest in this book—and for our conversations over cocoa—and for Bunnies.

❧ Special thank you to my *brother* Rev. Don E. Richards for his prayerful support and poems of encouragement, our conversations, and L.W.—and letters. And in loving memory of Romy (April 1996).

❧ My love and appreciation to Dennis and Patti Clancy—extended family—for love and support.

❧ For their encouragement and interest and prayers—thank you to all the "Muffins" of Immaculate Conception Church in Jenkintown, Pennsylvania.

❧ Thank you to special writer friend, Jeanie Quinn, for constant love, encouragement, and letters and love of animals.

❧ I am grateful to Janis Parks for her friendship, love, and letters—for devotion to God's creatures—and for reading my manuscript..

❧ In gratitude to Connie Gilman—friend, giver of animal books, calls, and love—for great giving of self to animals—and in loving memory of her beloved Tiger and Pretty Girl.

❧ To Bertha McDonnell for her love and spiritual friendship—and remembering forever in love Manny, Moses, and Jackie—beloved companion cats who passed away in 1996.

❧ And for my special friend and listener in New Hampshire, Clara Clark—I am grateful—and for her prayers. For our mutual love of little cats that we share, and for Jack—whose friendship matters.

❧ I am ever grateful to my healing music, "The Fairy Ring," on cassette tape by Mike Rowland, played during writing of this book.

❧ Special thanks to all those who contributed poems that appear in Appendix A: Poems for Meditation—Robert A. Kolb, Jr., Don Richards, Jessica Mae Kolb Drakely, June Leslie Kolb Hudson, Samuel Vincent Fasy, Jr., Peggy Dirvin, Francis Egan, Jane Michener Kroll, Barry Richard Greene, Laurel Elizabeth Kolb Gottlieb, Barbara Jan Kolb Egan, Janna R. Kolb VanDorick, and Julia Rose Hudson.

❧ And finally, I wish to thank all the authors of wonderful books about Animals and Animal Rights for the inspiration they have given to me.

May the words of this book—and the meditation of our hearts (the readers' and mine)—give glory to Our Lord—and love and gratitude to Blessed Mother Mary—who always intercedes.

Introduction

"*One does not meet oneself until one catches
the reflection from an eye other than human.*"
—Loren Eiseley

OR MANY YEARS NOW I have been experiencing a very extraordinary *truth. The closer that one comes to God and the longer one spends in His Presence in quiet and solitude—wordlessly just enjoying His Friendship and Love—the more one is filled with deepening compassion.* People and situations that once did not catch my attention, even though I have always tried to be very caring, now most certainly do have my involvement and help in ways that He leads. He seems to send many to me—even strangers—and they do not seem to be strangers when we encounter. Tears well up at the strangest times when I am alone, just merely thinking of a sadness or wound that someone is bearing, and in conversation with some, I find the tears there also, as we share deeply in Spirit or speak of others who need our help. The tears just spill out without warning, because He has put this inexplicable compassion within me, just as He has put it in the hearts of others. The outrageous accounts of suffering heard and seen on the news leave imprints on me, and memories of them I cannot shake. I pray! War is horrifying to me—that humans are killing each other and innocent children and others are slain in horrendous ways.

But when God places His deep compassion in a heart, it is not only for human beings; at least I have found this to be so. In recent years, my compassion for all God's creatures has increased to dimensions I never thought possible. I cannot bear to hear of any cruelty to any creature, no matter how large or how small. Animals and other living species—like the unborn of humans that are often senselessly aborted—have no voice. They are often tortured and killed mercilessly, as if they are incapable of pain. I am one of many who feel this is extremely wrong—and one who wants to be their voice.

In the past few years, a deep impression was put upon my heart to write about God's creatures and to reveal them in ways perhaps many have not considered. I know this impression came from His Spirit, for I have known such calls before and followed them.

The pages of this book contain deep personal sharings from my own life in regard to animals and also many true accounts of the experiences of others. Herein are truths to consider and reflect upon that you may not have known before, and scriptures to ponder in relation to animals. It is a book written mainly for Christians, but is essentially for anyone who wishes to take a new look at the creatures God placed into our care and to search his or her own heart in their regard.

Though I have loved many animals personally, one little feline in particular has changed my life. I know he was given to me by the One who put these stirrings within me, which would not leave—the stirrings that caused the writing of this book.

Those who know me well, know that when I love, I LOVE, and so perhaps you who do not know me may find the personal sharings of my relationship with my little cat quite unusual. But I have learned that many like myself will not find me "too strange" through the confessions I have made and the happenings in my life that I have been led to write down for all to see.

Living in the woods amongst nature on the shore of a lake has changed the way my husband and I view life. Wild little creatures come up onto our porch and peer through our sliding glass doors, and my little cat and they respond to each other through the screens or the glass. We have learned how intelligent these little beings are. We have seen them too outwit us—and been amazed. We have watched the interchange between birds and squirrels and chipmunks all feeding at the same bird feeders at the same moments. We have been surprised and overwhelmed by families of raccoons silently observing us through the glass, patiently waiting to search our faces and responses. We have watched the beautiful herons land in our cove and the families of ducks waddle up our beach to wait for us to feed them, so trustingly. Too, we have heard the incredible wail of the loons in day and night and observed them dive for food into the lake or run across the water. Nothing can compare to the lapping water and wail of the loon in the night.

The beaver has managed to stay out of sight, but he has freely let us know he is very much present. Though we have never seen one, we have been incredulous at the evidences of their close existence to us. Our first calling card from him (and perhaps his family as well) was the absence of two slender poplar trees on our property after we had been gone a week. We could see the teeth marks on the stumps and the tracks of beaver in the sand, and the tracks of tree branches that had obviously been dragged to the water. Our next evidence came several weeks later, when we could not open our door one morning because a tree was lying on the porch blocking it. Finally managing to get out, we knew again it was the work of the beavers. We never touched the tree, but each morning for the next week we would awaken to find more of the tree missing, until at last the entire tree had been taken away for use in the building of the beavers' home and dam. We found this whole event to be extremely interesting, and it caused us to read and learn more about beavers. I am sure they will call again, but it has been over a year since this last happening. We have hundreds of trees on our wooded property, so we certainly do not feel threatened by future loss. The beavers seem to select trees with thinner trunks. The shavings all about the ground, the very obvious teeth marks, and finally the gradual disappearance of the tree they took down while we were asleep, were all worthy of photos, which we did take. I have pictures of raccoons hanging over our highest birdfeeder at night—feasting well and with eyes gleaming red in the dark. I record the wildlife with my camera, as well as through keeping a wildlife log in a journal placed by the window with binoculars. We see foxes and opossums and rabbits in the woods—and rarely deer and moose. Osprey, mallard ducks, and other birds fly through in large migratory groups.

And in Spring and early Summer, when we open our windows, we hear a most supernatural harmony at twilight and throughout evening, until almost dawn, which I have termed "Nightsong." It is as if every animal, bird, and insect has joined voices, and this celebration is so incredibly beautiful and awesome to hear in the dark before sleep, or upon waking in the night. I somehow envision shafts of moonlight shining down through the trees into the woods, with this dear Creature Choir all assembled in the grasses and on branches and rocks, being directed by Snow White or a lovely Fairy Princess.

I put my watch aside and tell time by the sun's path across the sky as I write at my desk and night after night see God's sunsets on the lake. They never cease to inspire and leave me in awe, and almost daily I take pictures as the sun goes down. According to season, the color varies— and pink, orange, and red sunsets throughout the year continue to cast their spell of magical color over heaven and lake's surface and woods and myself.

Living enfolded in Nature in all seasons of the year—for, after this book was completed, we moved here permanently to the woods—gives one a new perspective. The earth and trees and God's creatures are part of us, and I would not now even kill a bug or an ant. If they are found inside, they are carried outdoors carefully. My husband has built a pro-life mouse trap, and if a little mouse enters it, tempted by the offering of jelly bean or peanut butter within, then he is caught. The trap looks like a little house, and I have decorated the outside to look like a home, at my husband's request. After greeting the little mouse within, he is taken outside in his house, and the door is opened and he is set free. Perhaps he runs right back into our cottage; we cannot be sure. But it really does not matter. He will find his way into the Mouse House once more. Life is good here, and I have come to realize that each life, no matter how insignificant it appears to human beings, IS A LIFE. I cannot kill. We live in peace and harmony here, and we let all else live in the same way.

There was a word that was not familiar to me until shortly before I began to write about God's creatures, when I was involved in reading about them concerning their treatment by the various religions of our world. I learned the word "*Ahimsa*," which means "harmlessness" or not hurting, and that it is a Sanskrit word for *compassion*. Wherever *Ahimsa* is found, there is deep compassion, unselfishness, and service to others, and a refraining from causing pain and suffering to any living creature. It naturally implies non-killing. In the numerous books in which I came upon the true meaning of this word, I also learned in each that to not cause injury truly means total abstinence from causing ANY harm or pain whatsoever to ANY living creature, either by thought, word, or deed. It is LOVE! Universal Love! In the long ago it was said that *Ahimsa* was prescribed by very wise men to eliminate cruel and brutal tendencies in man.

Ahimsa is said to be the highest and noblest of traits. To sum up all that *Ahimsa* is, is to learn that *Ahimsa* or non-violence has proven to be a great and mighty *Spiritual* force.

It is a trait that most surely we would desire in all religions. It is a word and subject that must be brought forth here to reflect upon as one continues now to read this book. It is a word and a teaching that I find essential to my life as a Christian and one that will remain with me as I strive to live it out. Its influence only deepens, and it is firmly entrenched in the compassion that Our Lord placed within my heart for humans and animals alike.

Please prayerfully investigate further and allow His Light to penetrate your mind and heart as you read—the same Light that brought all of this to light in my soul and caused me also to investigate and then to write down all that I was shown and all the personal joys I have been experiencing since sharing my life with one of His furry little children.

These writings have been covered with prayer from beginning to end—and I personally pray that the Holy Spirit will guide you lovingly through the reading of them, just as He has guided me through the writing.

—J.G.K.
Higher Ground on Lake Balch
E. Wakefield, New Hampshire

In loving memory of two beloved companions

Molly (Hudson)

Stuffy (Drakely)

PART ONE

❧

My Spiritual Education by Rochester the Cat

"Friendship is a union of spirits, a marriage of hearts,
and the bond thereof of virtue."
—William Penn

On June 23, 1986 Our Lord placed a gift down for me on a bench in a small mall in Rochester, New Hampshire. I did not know this gift was to be bestowed on me that day or on any day of my life, for this particular gift was one I had been forbidden to have for thirty-two years. Therefore—when it was placed there in a carton and all obstacles were removed from my being permitted to accept it—I was able to receive this gift with great, inexpressible joy. A few years later, words still cannot convey the depth of the joy that this gift has brought into my life. Only those who have been given a similar gift at some point in their lives can truly understand—and yet not quite so—for each gift is so utterly unique.

His gift of love that warm June morning took the form of a tiny marmalade and white furry kitten approximately eight weeks old. He was free—as is our Lord's love. All we need to do is accept His love. And so I accepted that indescribable gift of love—and in doing so I have felt the Lord's love to me more vividly with every passing day.

1

Who could have known my life would be changed so by the acceptance of this unexpected gift! In His perfect timing He brought me to that very spot in the mall to receive His love in a new way. There is a beautiful quotation by an unknown author that has come to mind again and again since this wonderful creature has become my inseparable companion:

> *God never loved me in so sweet a way before. 'Tis He alone who can such blessings send. And when His love would new expressions find, He brought thee to me and He said—Behold a friend.*

This is what our Lord had done for me! I am eternally grateful, and just as I am incapable of truly expressing the joy I feel—neither can I truly express my gratitude. I plead daily to Him to look into my heart and there He will find the joy and the gratitude bubbling over. He knows. It is written that *"Our deepest feelings live in words unspoken."*

I cannot now ever imagine my life without Rochester. Yes, Rochester. He is named for the town in which I received him and adopted him—and I felt it might possibly be the town in which he was born. He is also known affectionately by the shortened version of his name—"Chester."

And so—life is different now. A beautiful creature of God lives with me, sleeps with me, and spends the majority of his hours near me or on my lap—and my life is enriched because of him. I see with new spiritual eyes matters I did not see vividly and with my whole heart before. He has changed my husband's life and the lives of my friends—and I can no longer keep all of this to myself. One small cat has turned my existence upside down and caused me to reflect on numerous things, which before June 23, 1986 were not foremost in my thinking. I had to be gently shown, in love, and daily educated by a most unusual teacher in order for my attention to be drawn more and more in this direction. And it has been a Christian education.

Let me tell you what I have been taught in this "School of Love" by Rochester. But first let me share with you the details of this mutual adoption and our first days together.

CHAPTER ONE

❧

We Meet, and the Angels Sing!

"I love these little people: and it is not a slight thing when they, who are so fresh from God, love us."
—Charles Dickens

THE BLACK AND WHITE VAN pulled into the very large parking lot of a very ordinary little mall in Rochester, New Hampshire. It was late morning of a bright and beautiful day in June, and my husband and I smiled and commented on the blessing of our safe arrival. We slowly opened the doors and slid down from our seats and out of the van. Our teenage daughter, Janna, rolled gracefully out from the side door with her curly hair going in various directions and her expression still one of drowsiness. We had travelled through the night from our home in Pennsylvania, and this stop was only to quickly buy groceries. We would take them with us to our cottage on Lake Balch, some twenty-five miles further north.

As we entered the mall we were immediately confronted with a father and two children sitting on a round bench outside the supermarket and holding a sign proclaiming, "Free Kittens." Next to them on the bench was a closed carton. My daughter and I, upon encountering this sight, widened our eyes in a spontaneous secret signal to each other, without my husband realizing what was about to befall him.

Now, lest you begin to feel sorry for my husband, let me hurriedly take you back many years in order to understand the scene that has been unraveling before your eyes. I had been born into a home with a cat and had grown up with cats. Until I married and left home, exactly upon turning twenty-one years, I had had the joy and companionship of cats. But the day I married Bob, he said emphatically, "No Cats!"

In my thirty-two years of marriage I had loved and reared six children—five wonderful daughters and a fine son. I had also loved and cared for three hardy and adorable little Cairn Terriers and all the puppies of their many litters.

There had also been hamsters during those thirty-two years, and guinea pigs, mice, turtles, gerbils, fish—and one hermit crab that was lost in our home.

All of these, but my husband had said, "No Cats!"

Occasionally, throughout these many years, I had asked if I might have a kitten. More recently our daughter Janna had voiced the same request. Always the answer came back, "No Cats!"

Ah, but this day in the mall in New Hampshire, some supernatural power took over within me as I made my first pleas to Bob, in order that Janna and I might have one of these free kittens. When his usual reply came back to me, accompanied by the expression on his face that I well recognized, I would not be silenced! I asked again. Again. AGAIN. I began to frighten myself in my persistence, which refused to buckle under his rising anger and stormy appearance. I could not quiet my pleas until I at last, after thirty-two years, had won my simple request. Nothing else mattered in those moments but a "yes." I could never again bear to hear "No Cats!"

"All right, all right, get one, but I'll have nothing to do with it," he hissed. I began to say a continuous stream of "thank yous" and ran off to find my daughter, who had delicately removed herself earlier from the muffled battle scene. Oh, the joy and excitement of the two of us as we stifled squeals of victory between us, there in the aisle of the supermarket.

I, delirious with happiness, told my daughter to quickly go and pick out a kitten before her father changed his mind. I then dashed about the store to complete the shopping in a flash, with the hope of assuaging Bob's anger by my promptness.

Janna rushed back to find me. "Male or female?" she said. "Female, I suppose—perhaps easier to train." "But the little boy is so cute," said Janna. "He likes me!" "Get the boy then, quickly," I said and finished the shopping with a final toss of kitty litter and cans of cat food into the basket.

I pushed the cart of groceries to the van and waiting husband, and Janna carried the carton that contained our treasure. Peeking out whenever he could push his tiny head through was a beautiful pale orange and white kitten. Oh, I was ecstatic! Somehow I had expected to see a black cat like my cats had been years ago, and so the lovely light fur of this new kitten surprised me! He was perfect! My daughter sat in the seat behind, holding the carton as we drove, and the tiny face would pop out and look around. "I won't have a cat that is not clean!" stormed Bob. We drove further, with Janna and I sneaking glances at each other while adoring the kitten. "I don't want to have to listen to a lot of meowing!" Bob said, as we drove further. "This cat will be nothing but trouble!" he continued, "And what will we do with him when we travel?"

Silence took over for a bit, and then I suggested we give our sweet kitten a name. After several were thrown about to digest, it struck me that "Rochester" would be a fine name, after the town in which we had adopted him. It was voted a yes! Suddenly the man said, "Call him Chester for short." My daughter and I agreed and exchanging glances made no comment that her father had temporarily softened and joined in our joy. Once in our cottage and the little litter box was prepared, the tiny Chester jumped in to test it, thereby setting a pattern of faithfulness. From that moment on, he never gave Bob cause to accuse him of uncleanliness. He never made a mistake.

Soon we realized we had a very silent new family member, for Rochester never meowed. He spoke only from that day forward with his big loving golden eyes, which matched his fur, and he padded and ran about softly on his little white marshmallow paws. He was so grateful to be ours! He would never be trouble! He obviously wanted Janna and me to be proud of him, and he never gave cause for the man to be angry.

Each evening this dear little cat curled up on me as I slept, finding warm and comfortable places upon me to sleep throughout the night. One morning upon awakening, I saw my kitten lying across the forehead of my husband as he lay on his back beneath the covers. I said nothing of this but spoke to Bob as if a kitten was not upon his forehead. He replied in like manner as I left the room. How hysterical it was to talk to him with Rochester on his face! I ran to the next room and burst into laughter! It was better left alone and unremarked upon. I did not want to make Bob feel foolish, and I was so anxious that they come to know each other. This scene was often repeated from that day on.

As the days passed in the little cottage and Chester gave and gave his love to his new family, Janna and I soon began to hear:

"Hi, Harry!"

"Is your dinner good, Harry?"

"Where's Harry?"

Not able to express it, my husband had given our little cat another name, his secret way, perhaps even surprising and inexplicable to himself, of showing a special affection for the tiny kitten. And oh, how Chester proved he could travel and not be trouble to this man! In the first year of his life alone, Rochester made fifteen trips from New Hampshire to Pennsylvania and back, travelling the entire ten hours each trip on my lap.

All the words in the world from my daughter and I to convince Bob to accept the kitten were now not needed. The clean, obedient little Chester, with his gift of continual silence and unconditional love, had warmed Bob's heart and won for "Harry" his own acceptance.

*Rochester
as a kitten.
He has always
loved books!*

CHAPTER TWO

❧

The Bonding Ritual

"We do not need words
Our eyes speak—
Our touch reveals
Each new day we discover new beauty
In silence
Of each other."
—Walter Rinder

JUST AS HE WAS GENTLY SHOWING BOB loving secrets in the course of each day, Rochester selected an evening when the two of us were all alone, to teach me about "bonding." Three days after he came to live with us, everyone had gone to bed, and as I sat on the sofa in our small cottage on Lake Balch, my little Rochester slept beside me, curled up tightly. Soon he wakened and stretched his tiny little body and looked directly into my eyes. That alone struck my soul, this meeting of our eyes in the silence of the room.

Suddenly he came over onto my lap and sat there momentarily, continuing to look at me. I was so moved by his beauty and felt his closeness in a new way. Then something almost mysterious took place, and I have never forgotten it, nor the feeling that it enkindled within me. Often when I think back on it, I have tears and am "held" in a strange way as I reflect on it.

This tiny creature literally walked up the front of me and, with his tiny face just opposite mine, bumped his small forehead to the front of mine, several times. Then he climbed onto my right shoulder and went behind my neck, partially on me and partially on the sofa back. He began to play with my small gold hoop earrings, and I felt his paws on my head as he nestled his face into the back of my hair. Then he appeared on my left shoulder, rubbing into the side of my cheek. Down he went onto the front of my shirt, and then turned around once again to face me. Again he came up face to face with me, and again he bumped his little forehead into mine several more times. No sound was made, simply this meeting of our heads and minds.

Again he went onto my right shoulder and repeated all he had done before, playing with my earrings and hair. Again he appeared on my left shoulder. Once more he went through all he had done the first two times, the bumping of our heads and the nestling behind my head to play with earrings and hair, then down to my lap. When his eyes met mine this time, I knew in my heart that a most significant event had just transpired. It had almost been a little ritual, this exact repeat, three times, of bumping his head to mine, and then little displays of affection as he made his way behind my neck to circle around again.

This was something mystical to me. It was not an ordinary happening. Something deep within myself assured me that Rochester and I were bonded in a most unique way. I would go over and over it in my mind, that such a tiny little one repeated such a loving act three times and had communicated to me through this act and the love in his eyes that he had "somehow" made me "his." It was not until several weeks later, upon reading a wonderful book about cats, that I learned that "head bumping" is indeed a treasured happening between cat and human. It is the cat's way of telling his loved one that they belong to each other, that the human is the "cat's person," and the cat belongs to "that person." But actually, it is more so that the cat owns the person, and from that moment on a faithfulness remains. Certainly, in our relationship, Rochester and I have been eternally bonded and a most loving and spiritual relationship exists. He is mine and I am his, and he does not mind that all in his small world are informed of this.

Without my knowing that such a bonding is given by a cat when he has chosen his human, my tiny Rochester had made known to me, through his loving ritual and eyes that held me fast, that something on another plane was indeed taking place. He had even chosen a time of silence, when we were totally alone, for this marriage of hearts between kitten and human.

🐾

Some I have shared this story with have smiled and dismissed it with an amusing comment or with one showing no understanding, perhaps because they know my great love for my little cat, and they probably felt I had gone just a little overboard this time. Others receive it completely, knowing almost as well as I how tender and endearing the experience was. Dag Hammarskjold has written:

> *Never for the sake of peace and quiet deny your own experience or convictions.*

And I never shall! I am owned by a little cat!

Rochester (in "Pawtucket" position)

CHAPTER THREE

🐾

Breaking the Language Barrier

*"The greatest gift we can give one another
is rapt attention to one another's existence."*
—Sue A. Ebaugh

SENDING KISSES

Across the room his eyes meet mine
And capture them in fond embrace.
And I blink twice in sweet response
Twice kiss his furry little face.

For eyelids slowly closed and raised
Are kisses to a little cat—
He sends them back with golden eyes—
And bonds me to him just like that!

For those who dwell within this realm—
Of creature love and friendship dear—
Know it is a gift from God
That keeps His Presence ever near.

One evening, as Rochester sat on the table halfway across a room from me, "kisses" such as those described in the poem above took place; then, no longer being able to bear the distance, he joined me to curl up on my lap. I learned of this "kissing" phenomenon in cat communication from a wonderful book called *The Natural Cat*, by Anitra Frazier. From the first moment I read it, I put it into practice, and Rochester and I confirmed all she had written about "sending kisses." It is a very tender encounter, one I cherish, and this particular tryst that October evening seemed worthy of a poem with dedication to my Chester.

As I blink my eyes slowly to Chester, I always do as Anitra suggested and think the phrase, "I love you." ("I" before the blink, "love" during, and "you" after the blink.) I have also thrown cat kisses to other cats I have met about town (though not in the same deep way I send them to Rochester), if I can be in eye contact with them. The responses have been there and have been varied and so sweet as I have tried to break the language barrier—and succeeded! One little cat, after such an exchange, looked surprised as he sat on the pavement staring at me in my car. As I got out of the car to visit a friend, the little cat then rolled over on his back to me in complete trust, a most unusual surrender to a stranger, and I stooped in trust also, to pat him. If you truly love your animal companions, there are many special means of growing into a very deep relationship. The animal is the greatest teacher, and if we spend time with our companions, we are taught by them in a quite natural way.

They truly do have methods of communicating with us, if we only give them our undivided attention and time. That does not mean they must monopolize or control us, but if we love them and wish to truly know them, then we have to give ourselves to them in order to be taught and to learn. One will find that the more one gives of self, the more one will be rewarded by the giving of deep love and affection by one's animal friend. The famous painter, sculptor, inventor, poet, animal rights activist, and vegetarian, Leonardo daVinci, who filled notebooks with passages that show his compassion for living creatures, wrote:

> In truth, great love springs from great knowledge of the beloved object, and if you know it but little, you will be able to love it only a little or not at all.

When I read that, I knew daVinci must have had a companion in his life like Rochester, and I learned of his great love of animals only after Rochester came into my life.

Being Available to Learn

So many tender things have been shown to me by my little friend, and I feel this is because I make myself available to be taught and because I truly want a deep relationship and a companion, not a pet. When I see he wants to be with me, indicated in various ways, then unless I am extremely busy, I give him my time. This is the usual, for I am a softie and cannot turn him away. It has to be a major happening, like my hair being on fire, before I would refuse Rochester from settling down on my lap. In fact, I have often postponed things I was just about to do, once he has stood on my lap, looked in my eyes, and curled up contentedly. And since I am making confessions, I have also stayed up much later than my usual outlandishly late hours, just because he was so absolutely precious in sleep that I could not bear to disturb him! With little head back and chin upturned and a white marshmallow paw over his nose as he is tightly circled on my lap, what is a girl to do? How could I disturb him? And so I often write into the wee hours of the morning with a legal pad balanced on the arm of my chair, or finish reading a book in those hours that I did not think I would be able to finish for several days! This is what love can do! Yet all I would have to do is momentarily disturb him to lift him to the bed, for that is where he spends every night on my legs. I was feeling a little bit guilty for my extreme love and patience, until I read that a very well-known spiritual leader actually cut the sleeve from his garment in order not to disturb his sleeping cat!

I am not saying one has to go to the extreme in order to be in a loving relationship with one's animal companion, but I do feel there is a giving of self necessary. I am extreme in many areas of my life, so in a thing of such magnitude as my companionship with my little cat, for whom I waited patiently for thirty-two years, then I beg your indulgence for some of my idiosyncrasies, yet encourage you to root out the worthwhile, the sensible, and above all the loving suggestions and lessons in this book, such as those I have been taught by Rochester. You see, I am willing to work here at my desk with my dear little guy actually lying on the very papers I am writing upon, while I gently pull out each finished paper from under his body, or while he lies next to my papers on my small desk as I write. Yes, he is taking up valuable space, but what is more valuable—this little life, or a period of time working without encumbrances? I could never ask him to leave! Instead, after every several sentences I write, I pause to hug him and kiss his little face. His purring is my background music, and I feel like I am the most blessed person on earth to have such a "gift" sitting here before me and actually choosing to be with me.

Bob also experiences this when I am out of the home and he is working at his desk. Rochester will choose to sun himself in a tiny space under the desk lamp, thereby blocking the light and being very much in the way. But there he is allowed to remain! Or he will curl up on Bob's legal pad or book, or on the very writing area of the desk, just to be near Bob.

Author Theophile Gautier wrote comments about his cat that make me truly smile in understanding!

> *He loved books, and when he found one open on the table he would lie down on it, turn over the edges of the leaves with his paw, and after a while, fall asleep, for all the world as if he had been reading a fashionable novel.*

"Do Unto Others"

I have never treated Rochester with disrespect or impatience, and neither have my husband or daughter, Janna. When Chester enters a room, I greet him and call him little love names or ask how he is. No, this is not crazy; it is treating him with the same respect we ourselves like to receive. Bob usually says, "Hi, Harry!" (It is written that one who is loved is given many names.) Janna loves to roughhouse with him and often rumbles with him in gentle attacks; he loves it! But that is not how he and I relate, and each of us has our own way of showing our love to our little furry family member.

Learning from Others' Suggestions

Much can be learned from books written by authors who love animals and treat them with respect. I feel it is absolutely essential to purchase a book of worth when you acquire a new animal companion; though we are shown many things by our personal companion, many essential things can be learned from other animal lovers about the care and well-being of our animals. For example, I have found everything I needed to learn and an abundance of extra valuable knowledge in *The Natural Cat*. Though I have read many other books and still do, this book remains the ultimate for me, and I keep it nearby at all times. The author reminds me of myself in her extreme love of her cats and the affectionate ways in which she shares her life with them, besides grooming and tending other people's cats as well.

Among the many teachings in that book, one that has greatly helped Rochester and myself is in the section on feeding and nutrition, about the food and vitamins that are essential for the perfect healthy lifestyle that a cat is entitled to live. I follow her advice to the letter, and the results are excellent. Also through advice given in this book, my husband—the one who refused to allow a cat into our home for thirty-two years—designed and constructed the most magnificent scratching post that any little cat ever could hope to own. Bob freely worked diligently for several days in the basement, after reading a certain section of *The Natural Cat*. Then, with finished project in hand, he emerged from downstairs, and with an implied "TA-DAH," he presented it to Rochester, placing it in the middle of the living room floor. It was most wondrous—all covered with green carpet to match our New Hampshire cottage, and with strong ropes dangling from the four corners of the top portion, for Chester to chew and hang on. It was all a cat could hope for or dream of in a scratching post, and it also sported a lovely flat area on top for mere sitting upon. This scratching post was and is deeply appreciated, and to this day it is used pleasurably by little Rochester. It has a place in the living room and blends right in. Bob even put the carpet on wrong side out, for more scratching ability and toughness. It has everything! Need I repeat the specialness of a certain relationship between a man and his first cat, "Harry"?

Yes, life is good shared with this dear animal. Though he has bonded deeply with me and continues to, he also shows love always to Bob and Janna and enjoys their company. He also greets them and occasionally "head bumps" in soft, tender moments. He greets others who enter our home in a friendly way. Never has he hissed or shown any hostile behavior since the time he came to be with us. He is truly All Love.

A Love Ritual

When I return from daily Mass or other places, Bob tells me he knows well in advance when I will arrive, because Rochester knows and prepares for my arrival and stirs from whatever he is doing to greet me. When I come in the door of the kitchen, he bounces toward me on his little legs, as if he were a wind-up toy, and he makes a sound like the chirp of a bird. After I stroke him briefly, he runs to the family room, expecting me to follow, and there he lies down and stretches out as long as possible, waiting for me to join him on the floor. I invariably do, and I pet him and nuzzle his little neck and whisper sweet nothings in his ear and kiss his little face. Oh, he is in heaven! We repeat this several times. He gets up and lies down in a new location nearby. After this love ritual, we are free to talk and go about the house together. He taught me this! It was instinct in me to get down on the floor and be with him. For those of you who do the same, I know you understand. Later, I found mention in a book that this is a very tender ritual, with a picture of a little cat in this same position. The author had captioned it, "Be my love." And that is truly what Rochester is saying, and so I am, every time.

I can only repeat that giving of self is necessary to know our animal companions, for they, too, give themselves to us, if we are attentive and loving. Rochester loves each one of us in our family—each has a unique loving relationship with him—but there is only one whom he truly owns, it would seem, and that is the one who permits herself to be owned, to feed and care for him, and to bond again and again in ways he initiates and in ways I have learned also to initiate. Thus, I count my relationship with Rochester as a spiritual blessing from God, and I shall forever be "Sending Kisses."

CHAPTER FOUR

❖

Instruments of His Peace

*"Great truth that transcends nature does not pass from one being to
another by way of human speech. Truth chooses silence
to convey her meaning to loving souls."*
—Kahlil Gibran

NOT EVERYONE WILL UNDERSTAND when I say that my little cat brings
me closer to Our Lord. I have only to look at Rochester and I find
myself immediately thanking Jesus for the gift of this little one in my life.
This occurs many times a day, quick darts of prayer sent winging
heavenward to Him. For instance, as Rochester lies here on my desk as
I sit writing before my window in my "room with a view," I repeatedly
look out over the lake and up to the sky and say inwardly, "Thank you,
Jesus." It just happens! This little being's mere presence causes joyous,
grateful prayer to rise in me!

In the Presence of the Lord

I have also learned and experienced that Rochester comes to me,
even in the midst of something else he is doing, whenever I am praying.
This has happened over and over again, and each time it ends up with
him curled up in my lap. When I feel completely centered (as opposed
to scattered and pulled in many directions) and at peace within, then
Rochester becomes the outward symbol of that inner condition, for he
wants to be as close to me as he possibly can be. When I am holding him

quietly and I suddenly raise my voice to answer someone who has called me in the house—or someone comes in and talks loudly to me—he leaves my lap to go elsewhere, until the climate for peace and prayer and togetherness exists again. He is very quiet himself, a gentle little cat that reminds one of a contemplative. He loves quiet times with me—his mere presence causes prayer as he lies there, so beautifully curled on my lap, from time to time changing positions, with each position more adorable than the last. There is nothing I love more—except for sitting silently before the Tabernacle in Church following Mass—than to sit in total silence with Rochester on my lap in peace, in wordless prayer. Together we just enjoy the Lord's Presence.

Often, when I lie in bed or sit in a chair praying my Rosary, if he is not already on my lap, he is drawn to come to me. It touches my heart so deeply to see his tiny white paw reach out gently to pat the Rosary from time to time. He cannot resist the beads and often will keep part of the strand immobile for a time, as he places his paw on it and claims it for his own.

The Blessed Cat and the Christ Child

My little Rochester belongs to the Blessed Mother! I have come to know this through an account in a book, and whether it be legend or truth, I am a believer. It is written that the Baby Jesus was crying in His little manger in the stable, and His Mother could not get Him to sleep. One by one, each animal in the stable tried his best to calm the little baby. Suddenly, a little marmalade tabby cat jumped into the manger with the Christ Child and gently lulled the Tiny One to sleep with his soft purring. The Blessed Mother Mary, ever so grateful, blessed the little cat and placed the mark of an "M" on the forehead of this tiny helper—and to this day, that breed of cat bears the "M" as a mark of Mary. My little Rochester, too, has an "M" on his forehead, and it is no wonder, therefore, that he is drawn to my Rosary Beads!

Rochester Keeps a Loving Vigil

There have been times when I have not been feeling well, and without question Rochester knows this also and is ever there for me. He climbs up on my lap and stays there, for he knows something is amiss, and he knows he is a comfort to me. In the fall of 1989, I had a period of about a week or more when I was ill with breathing problems. I was not able to go to bed most nights, and if I did at all, I was forced to sit up. One night in particular, I felt extremely ill and very fearful, all due to breathing difficulties.

My husband covered me in my chair, and I sat there depending on the Lord above to in some way bring relief and remove the intense fear. We were in the woods and far from any help or hospital. As soon as I was covered, Chester jumped into my lap, and he looked into my eyes in such a way that it made me cry. I knew without a doubt that my companion knew I was ill and that I needed him very much. He circled into my lap and lay against me as firmly as he possibly could. And then he did something that touched me so deeply: he wrapped his little paw and arm about my hand in a firm hold, and he literally held my hand in his. He could not have held it more securely, had he been a human being. His "knowing" of my illness and fear is something I shall always remember.

He has done similar things at other times when I was not as ill as I was that night (actually I am rarely ill), but the Lord was evidenced to me all through the night, through Chester, who snuggled near and held my hand. At times he would stand, circle about, and lie down again, but always my hand was held fast. Sometime during the night, after hours of no sleep, I drifted off at last. When we woke together in the morning, I was well again at last.

Rochester with scratching post Bob made for him.

Settling In

Little furry face and head
An inch from mine—I lie in bed—
He stares into my eyes and purrs
Then walks my body—he prefers—
To settle down on legs awhile,
Then moves to tummy—he knows I'll—

Not move an inch—he's here to stay
Because he knows now that we'll pray—
I with my Rosary—now the beads—
Know too, sweet paws and purrs and kneads.
In union with the breaths I take—
He's lulled to sleep until we wake.

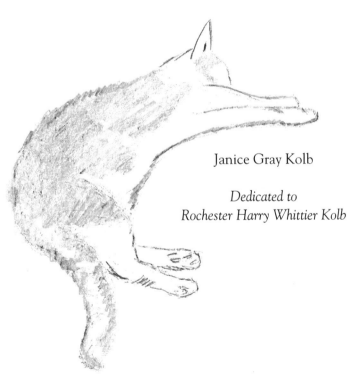

Janice Gray Kolb

Dedicated to
Rochester Harry Whittier Kolb

CHAPTER FIVE

Sacramentals

*"All creatures desire to speak God in their works: they all speak Him as
well as they can, but they cannot really pronounce Him."*
—Meister Eckhart (1260–1327, Sermons)

Wordless Adoration

Chester's actions are not only a delight but also true meditations
to me. My husband can be lying in bed reading a book, and Chester
will leave the comfort of my lap and walk up the front of my husband and
sit on his chest, directly in front of his book, so that he cannot read. He
sits there without a sound and stares into Bob's face. Who can resist this
little guy? He loves Bob, and he is not being obnoxious. He feels the
need to be given his attention, instead of the attention being given to
the book that is blocking his view of Bob's face and removing Bob's
thought from even thinking of Chester. To quietly sit in front of one you
love and tell him wordlessly you want his company is truly something to
think upon. It reminds me of myself, sitting wordlessly before the
Tabernacle in Church following Mass, having just received Our Lord in
the Eucharist. How sad I would feel if a barrier were placed between the
Tabernacle and myself! Some might feel angry at this interruption, but
because of Chester's gentle nature and his behavior that borders on
saintly, how can one be angry at him? He loves, and he shows it. Child-
like, he presents himself. I thank God repeatedly for such an utterly
precious creature.

Often, when I am working at my desk, with Chester lying quietly on it, suddenly he will spy an eraser or pencil that looks particularly appealing. His dear little white paw will begin to pat at it to move it, and if one could see the delightful motions he goes through with that paw and the expression on his face, it would be cause for saying, "Thank you, Jesus," just as I feel within me. Soon the object of his attentions is delicately patted off the end of my desk to the floor, and he sits watching it from on high, then lies down again, satisfied with what he has achieved. I sit just smiling and longing to hug him during it all, but I let him finish while I say my little prayer of gratitude.

A Model of Utter Trust

When he is lying on my lap asleep, with one little paw over his nose or eyes in utter trust, then I realize Our Lord is using him whom I care for so deeply to show me that I must have simple trust like this—to close my eyes and put myself into the care of the Lord in sleep, and to give myself to Him as I awake each morning, in that same simple trust. A beautiful quote by D. H. Lawrence reads:

> All that matters is to be at one with the Living God, to be a creature in the house of the God of Life. Like a cat asleep on a chair, at peace, in peace, and at one with the master of the house, with the mistress. At home. . . .

And this speaks of my Chester, asleep on my lap, asleep on the bed, one with God, one with us—at home.

Once about 2:30 a.m., while I was still awake, a poem came to me as I observed my small companion asleep on my legs. I quickly wrote it down, as it expresses portions of what I feel deep within my heart.

SLUMBER PARTY

I sit in bed to read and write,
He curls upon my legs each night.
To feel his warmth and goodness there,
Causes always silent prayer.

Dear small marshmallow paw of white
Across his eyes to shield the light.
My heart wells up to see his face—
Truly moments of sweet grace.

Just as we settle down to slumber,
Rochester plays his lullaby number.
His purring—satisfying and deep—
Lulls two friends right off to sleep.

Rochester as Sacramental

Holy cards and pictures and medals and statues and nature all lead me closer to God, and the presence of my Rochester is also a sacramental. His unending gaze upon a chipmunk's activities outside on the deck, or on the snowflakes falling as his little head follows repeatedly the descent of individual flakes, only to lift eyes upward again to help another fall to the ground, shows me that I too, must take time to see the wonders around me that God has placed there to inspire and uplift me. I must take time to smell the flowers and let the sacrament of the moment be nourished and absorbed and appreciated.

His kindness and gentleness in all situations speak to me, reminding me not to become undone and ruffled in the face of obstacles and indifference. When he sees us and wants to show instant love, he lies down and rolls on his back; with little paws bent and with his golden eyes, he beckons us to come to him and spend time with him. This reminds me that I too must surrender to Our Lord and give Him my time and undivided attention in love, just as Rochester desires that we give this to each other.

When he sits on his little feeding table, waiting with not a word to prod me on, just his quiet presence and loving gaze while I am busy at other things, then I realize his patience is a gift to me to inspire me in my own. His love is always there for me when I feed him, whether it be on time or whether I have unintentionally made him wait for an extended period. He loves me as I am, and that has always been difficult for me to believe of Our Lord. Even after I serve Chester his meal, he is not interested in it until we have first shown great affection and love to each other, which can at times mean play—or perhaps just my hugging him and holding him to me, or he may jump down from the feeding table to stretch out on the rug, which is an invitation for me to be with him there. To express to me in these ways that our relationship to each other comes before even his having physical nourishment is surely the dearest expression of his love. It is comparable to spending time in saying Grace before our meals in thanksgiving for the food and showing our love to the One who is back of the wind and the rain and the sun that caused our grains and fruit and vegetables to grow, which are now on the table before us. And so this dear little furry companion brings His Presence into our lives in very real and surprising ways at times—frequently and gently revealing God—suddenly and amazingly so! This quotation makes me smile, for it seems to have been written about my beloved little Chester:

> At dinner time he would sit in a corner concentrating, and suddenly they would say, "Time to feed the cat," as if it were their own idea.
>
> —Lilian Jackson Braun

Lessons in Play and Relaxation

Everything that moves serves to interest and amuse a cat, and whether it be the tiny ants he nestles by on the floor to watch intently for a half hour, the boughs of a tall tree swaying, or a boat going by, Rochester's observations tell me that I, too, must be aware of those that move about me, whether in home or Church or among friends or strangers or our animal friends, and see what He is saying through these others. Am I to be simply an observer, or am I to reach out and touch and make myself known—as Rochester does on occasion to the little ants. That pat is not meant to harm, but to say, "I am here." Perhaps that is all Our Lord wants at given times, just a touch or a pat upon another life to say, "I am here."

When it is time to make the bed each morning, it takes twice the time and more, because this is major playtime for Chester. Often he is waiting on the bed, sitting behind a mound of sheets and blankets, so that I can see only his ears and his bright eyes staring at me. He is waiting to play our game—the one that he created. Other times, he races to the bed the minute he sees me headed in that direction, and then the game begins. No matter what the approach, the object is for him to dive under the sheets, and I tickle and rustle his little body about while he is totally covered. He grabs onto my hand through the sheets but never to hurt me. He has never hurt me in anyway at any time! He makes little paths under the sheets, and I follow his moving body to accost him lovingly again. He just cannot get enough of this! Then, when I gently pull the sheet back over his face to expose it when I end the game, we nuzzle heads and give mutual affection. Often he will wait at the bedroom door, no matter what time of day, if I am near it, and then with eyes looking straight into mine to give directions, he races in on top of the made bed, waiting for me to come in and have some roughhouse with him. He could not say it any more clearly if he could speak: that I am to follow and that he has plans for us. Again, he is teaching me to play and be child-like, even in the midst of a busy day. What can it hurt—and in the end, only those loving moments are remembered, and not that I took a mini-break.

Frequently, Chester sits before the television set and becomes totally absorbed in a program. He seems to favor basketball, like his "Dad," or the wildlife programs, but he watches other things at times. What delight, to see him absorbed in a basketball game, his little head moving about to watch the action. It is really humorous to watch him from behind. When a ball bounces about on screen and suddenly comes to the foreground to disappear off camera, Rochester has actually looked about next to him on the floor, believing it came right out at his feet. Often I feel guilty if I watch television in evening without a pen in hand or open book, but I believe Our Lord is allowing Chester to show me the delights of just relaxing and enjoying a show. It is good for us to unwind. And when I do get comfortable, then he jumps up and spends the time that I give to this leisure, curled in a circle on my lap.

In so many ways, we learn from our animal companions, and the lessons are always given in such love and delight that, yes, we are drawn closer to our Lord. For me, the delight is the constant "thanking" within for His gift of Chester. I feel gratitude continuously!

CHAPTER SIX

❧

Companions on Retreat

"Music I heard with you was more than music and
bread I broke with you was more than bread."
—Conrad Aiken

IN THE MONTHS PRECEDING AND FOLLOWING my adoption of Rochester, there was much sadness in my life. There had been the unexpected death of a beautiful friend, which came suddenly, four days after the adoption of Rochester, from a heart attack. Though she had cancer, we had not expected her death at this point, and memories of days spent with her alone as I cooked macrobiotic meals for her would flood my mind. We could not speak together, as she was Peruvian, and I had limited Spanish and she did not know any English. Yet, we spent days communicating heart-to-heart, eye-to-eye, and with loving gestures— and the weeks and months of aloneness with my lovely friend would come over me, and I could not shake the sadness.

Also there were other happenings in my life at that time, a betrayal by a friend and other smaller, hurtful situations, and I fell into a depressed and sad condition, and I could not seem to rise above this. At last, I came to the decision that I must go away alone to our cottage in the wood. This is something I had never done before but had always dreamed of doing. I was inspired to do this through the reading of a book that influenced me greatly, called *An Unknown Woman*, by Alice Koller. Alice had gone to Nantucket in mid-winter with her new puppy as companion, to search out in solitude the meaning of her life. And so,

I too went away, but to the woods of New Hampshire, with Rochester as my only companion. I could not remain there for four months as Alice had done on Nantucket, for she was single, while I had family responsibilities and so could remain only one week. Nevertheless, this was a monumental event for me. I went to the woods, like Thoreau, to investigate my life and to find healing, and as Alice Koller did, I too wrote a book about this experience, as a guide and help to others, under the title of *Higher Ground*. But the point here is that the joy of having my tiny furry companion with me is almost impossible to express. We did it together, and it was a further deep bonding, and I am still thankful for this Retreat.

His Love Helps Me Heal

To have Rochester with me in the woods was a consolation, for he was someone to talk to and to comfort and to care for. It was a most unusual week in the cottage together. It was a solitude that is difficult to explain. He was there in everything I did, adding enjoyment to my days and comfort to my heart when I was sad. He was there to hold and to cuddle with when I was frightened by outside noises at night, and it gave me great joy to feed him and play with him. He was there for me, waiting each morning when I returned from Mass.

So many times when I was sad or upset and was reading or praying or writing, I would look up to see where he had gone, and I would suddenly spy him sitting in the kitchen sink, across the room, with just his tiny little head peering above. That was all I could see—his dear little face and those big golden eyes looking at me! It made me want to go over and hug him, and I often did. I would leave a carton on the floor and a paper bag—and when not sitting on my lap or curled next to me sleeping, he would play in the bag or carton. His favorite toys then and now were the soft plastic circlets that one peels off the tops of gallons of milk, and these gave him endless enjoyment—tossing them and chasing them and carrying them to other parts of the cottage in his mouth. I believe my retreat would not have been as it was, if I had not had Rochester with me. He gave me such a feeling of security and much love and comfort, and he was cause for thankfulness to our Lord continuously.

I would sit on the sofa with my books near by and my journal on my lap, writing down moments from my retreat or thoughts and reflections, in an attempt to come through the problems and my inner pain and sadness—and Chester would jump up and sit squarely on the pages of my journal and look into my face. I will never forget those moments. Or he would curl right up on the open pages and settle down for a nap. Would I move him? No. At first I would gently lift him to one side next to me, and in an instant he would be back onto the journal. And so he would stay—because I preferred him there over any possible thing I could put on those pages. He was more likely to bring healing to me than anything else that found its way onto those blank sheets!

It was also a sweet thing to realize that the very sofa I sat upon—and which Rochester played on, curled up on, and simply sat upon to observe the surroundings—was the very same sofa I had sat upon as a teenager and young woman of twenty, with my former cat of my growing up years. She was a black angora named Mitzi, and I loved her. She was always with me. Even as I had sat upon this sofa at the age of twenty-one, expecting my first child, Mitzi was by my side or on my lap. After my parents' deaths within one year of each other, we brought their living room sofa and chair to our cottage in the woods, and there it has stayed. So, on that retreat and even now as I write, my precious Rochester enjoys the same sofa as the cat of my growing up years—and that is rather amazing, when I think of it, for at the time I had been married thirty-five years!

Rochester in sink on retreat

Rochester in bag on retreat

CHAPTER SEVEN

❖

Channel of Love

"God made all the creatures
And gave them our love and our fear.
To give sign, we and they are His children,
One family here."
—Robert Browning (1812-1889)

*I*T IS QUITE POSSIBLE that I would not have gone away alone if I had not had Rochester. Looking back, I see how the Lord allowed first his entrance into my life, and then gave me the courage to go away. It was never even a passing thought that Rochester should remain in Pennsylvania without me. I had known since he first became mine (or I became his) that he would always be with me. I could never go away without him. Our Lord truly made Chester an instrument in my life for healing and courage.

I also have come to realize that he was the instrument and muse for my writing two books. The first book, *Higher Ground*, concerns the retreat in the woods that we made alone together. Following this retreat, I began to write about it in a short story form, from my memories and through the use of the journal that I had kept. Once I began writing, the short story grew into a full length book, for the writing of it had been therapy and had helped to bring healing and a desire to help others through the openness of my writing. I am convinced that Chester's presence gave me courage to go away, and later also to write about it. Aside from the chief desire for helping others through this book, I wanted to pay tribute to Chester's life, which has enriched mine and aided me in so many ways, most especially by his unconditional love.

And now, another book is being written because of Rochester and to honor his being—and his presence to me—and again, I pray that it will help others, and that is my chief desire.

And so, this beautiful marmalade and white creature has become an Ambassador for Christ, just as scripture states we all must be. As he continued to be a channel of Jesus' Love to me—and then to Bob—he soon became one to others, in a gradual and unassuming way. Because of my letter-writing ministry and interest in healing and encouragement of others, inspired by the Holy Spirit, I began at times to send cards and notes with Rochester's name signed to them, instead of my own. I did this when a friend or acquaintance was ill for an extended period and confined to a longer recovery. Since I almost daily sent little messages, to lighten hearts and bring in a small change from the more serious topics, I would often send instead a card from Rochester. He was always respectable in addressing my friends and would never call them by their first names. Sometimes he might write, "Dear Mistress Charlotte" or "Aunt Ruth" or "Mister Ed" or "Friar Francis." Soon his personality became more real to the recipients, as he would share little personal tidbits of his life in the notes. Also, I would share about him continu-ously with my friends. Over the few years of his young life, he has warmed and changed some hearts, and also some human views toward animals. One of his most beloved pen pals is "Mister Ed," and during many times of confinement in hospital and home, Rochester would write him or send over tiny remembrances to make him smile. When he was well, my friend "Mister Ed" came to me in church at daily Mass one day and smilingly said, "Will you thank my friend Rochester for me? And I have never even shaken paws with him!" This was so tender, and I have never forgotten it.

I believe other friends now have somewhat of a different outlook on life as it can be shared with animal companions, and their love and intelligence, after my speaking of life with Rochester so naturally and all the joy he brings us all continuously. People have shared with me that they have rethought their former views. A close friend, Ruth, always had a fear of animals, because she had been frightened as a child by a dog. But she turned out to be the one most interested in hearing my little

daily stories about Rochester, over coffee after Mass. She enjoyed
pictures of him and soon began giving me gifts with cat motifs, the first
being a beautiful cat calendar. These gifts continue, and she gets as
much joy in giving as I do in receiving them. I, too, then began to give
similar things, as her love for animals grew. Gradually, a beautiful thing
happened. Not only did she passively begin to change, but she began to
talk to the dog next door to her, confined in its yard. This was a
monumental happening, for Ruth had been afraid of the dog. As the
weeks and months have passed, Ruth has continued her greetings to
"Sandy" each time she goes out and passes her yard, and what is more,
she now puts her hand through the fence to pat her and also plays ball
with her! Sandy brings the ball back to Ruth, so happy to have her as a
new friend. As this continues, Ruth has also been attentive to a stray cat
that made its home in her yard. She is caring and concerned and quite
fond of her new charge. She often expresses amazement at herself and
the transformation of her being in this area of animals. And she always
lovingly attributes it to Rochester, that he helped her become open to
change and healing. She has also been so helpful to me during the
writing of this book, due to her saving of articles concerning animals,
which she comes across in newspapers or periodicals.

I had a beloved friend (and still do, though he resides in Heaven),
an elderly retired obstetrician. He was a poet and a very Holy man.
Because of our mutual love of Thomas Merton, a Trappist Monk who
once lived in The Abbey of Gethsemani in Kentucky and whom we
believed was responsible for our meeting and becoming friends at daily
Mass, I called him "Friar Francis," and he named me "Trappistine Jan."
It was a "love part" of our very spiritual friendship. In the last three years
of our extremely close five-year friendship, Friar Francis came to love
animals because of Rochester. Until then, he had never had a relationship with an animal or thought about them in a significant way. As time
passed and we talked more concerning the animals, he could not believe
that he had neglected them so in his thinking—though not deliberately—as he was actively pro-life and everything he did in life was to
give new life to others, in the years of his medical practice, his prison
ministry at Graterford Prison, and his arduous efforts to blot out
abortion. He enjoyed our conversations and all the notes Rochester
would send. He also read with love and concern the poems I wrote about

animals. When I came to visit him immediately after becoming a vegetarian, he was in awe. This caused even deeper conversation. He said he would have gladly given up his way of eating had he been the cook. But because of his confinement and the generous help he received from several friends cooking his meals, he could not at this point change his diet. But it now caused him to reflect on matters that he never had before. He was suddenly overcome by the wisdom that the same Lord who had breathed life into his body, breathes it into the animals, and that we are created in the exact same way as God's creatures. He even had a rubber stamp made (one of many) for my letter-writing ministry, to stamp onto each envelope. I use it every day. It reads: *"Life Is Love's Breath Inspiriting Creation."*

At one point I took him a framed 5x7 picture of Rochester next to a bouquet of flowers, because Friar Francis was not well enough to come to my home to meet Rochester personally. He loved the picture and kept it on his bureau among his Holy Pictures. When in the last months of his life he was forced to go to a nursing home, Rochester's picture went with him and remained close by his bed in his room until he died. Truly Rochester brought him joy. He enjoyed hearing about him, and through this continual sharing he was thankful to have come to a love of animals. The following poem expresses my experience of my precious friend, Friar Francis.

SPIRITUAL FRIENDSHIP

Like immortality of soul
Your friendship is perceived
By one who treasures each as gift
Too good to be believed.

Once in an age God sends to us
A friend of infinite worth—
All love and kindness—good and true
Heaven upon earth.

These are only several instances of Rochester being a channel for God's love to others and "an instrument of Peace"—a phrase the great animal lover St. Francis of Assisi used in his well-known prayer. Read this prayer now for the first time or read it anew, but read it perhaps in light of a new relationship to God's wonderful creatures that share the world with us, and ponder what you personally may possibly be able to do for them.

THE PRAYER OF SAINT FRANCIS

Lord, make me an instrument of Thy peace; Where there is hatred let me sow love; Where there is doubt, faith; Where there is despair, hope; Where there is darkness, light, and where there is sadness, joy.

O Divine Master, grant that I may not so much seek to be consoled as to console; to be understood, as to understand; to be loved, as to love; for it is in giving that we receive, it is in pardoning that we are pardoned, and it is in dying that we are born to eternal life.

Then miracle shall follow miracle, and wonders shall never cease.

—St. Francis of Assisi

Rochester with snow storm behind him

CHAPTER EIGHT

❖

A Tragedy and a Turning Point

"The natural world is the larger sacred community to which we belong.
To be alienated from this community is to become destitute
in all that makes us human."
—Father Thomas Berry

ANY MAY NOT EMBRACE THE THEOLOGY of our animal companions inhabiting Heaven, but scripture is written to support this idea, and light and comfort is given to the hearts who have loved their devoted animal friends and grieved deeply over their passing. There is a blessed "knowing" within, given by Our Lord, of this truth, that our precious companions, He created to enrich our lives on earth, will share Heaven with us and await us.

I had many animals in my life before Rochester, as mentioned in a previous chapter. Seven of these—three cats and four dogs—I loved in a serious way. Their existence mattered deeply to me, and when they were gone I was saddened, not casually or briefly, but as if I had lost true friends. I did not grieve for several days and then forget, but to this day their memories affect me. My three cats over the span of my first twenty-one years had a special place in my heart because I was an only child. After marriage, three Cairn terriers were with me constantly for sixteen years. When these three little hardy and loving dogs died, we did not bring another animal companion immediately into our home. Our dogs had been a joy but also a great responsibility while rearing six children, for everywhere our family travelled, our three terriers travelled with us in the van. They were a complete part of us.

We were not expecting one of our daughters shortly afterwards to ask if she could have a dog of her own—one to care for and be hers alone. Since she was a loving and responsible teenager, we gave our consent. Jessica already was interested in a certain litter of puppies, and so she obtained a lovely female puppy, a beautiful blonde, and her friend Michael (later to become her husband) adopted a sister, an auburn-colored puppy. The puppies were not only different in color but very different in personality. Michael's female puppy became a tom-girl, because she was accustomed to Michael's way of living, and Jessica's puppy became like Jessica, very feminine.

Jessica, so completely feminine, cared for her puppy as if she were a child. She spoke to her like a daughter and expected obedience. She showered her with love, and her time and attention, and she took Katie everywhere that she possibly could. From the moment of Katie's entrance into Jessica's life, to see Jessica was to see Katie. The puppy slept with her, roomed with her, and had her own rack upon the wall that held her increasing collection of gaily colored scarves.

Each morning, Jessica tied a scarf about her "daughter's" neck, not in bandana-style like a boy would sport it, but in a girlish bow. Katie was so proud of this and would go bounding through the house to show the rest of her family the scarf she had been dressed in for that day. All would exclaim over her bow, and she knew she was a "little girl" and looked very pretty. If a special occasion arose, Jessica would change her scarf, just as a mother would change the dress of a child.

The beautiful blonde coloring of this lovely miniature Collie/Labrador combination added to the inner beauty of Katie's loving personality. Under her eyes were thin, delicate, dark lines, which gave the appearance of makeup. Family often teased that Katie wore eye liner. She was true femininity, a reflection of her "Mother," Jessica.

She knew right from the beginning of her life with this loving Mother that she was a "person." She was treated with kindness and respect, and the first inkling that she was so deeply loved came when

Jessica gave her the beautiful "person" name of Katherine Elizabeth. She also knew each family member by name and if instructed to go to one, that one would find Katie promptly before them, enthusiastically making her presence known.

I had a blue and white prayer room, filled with my spiritual keepsakes, and this quiet place was a favorite of Katie's, as companion there to her "Grandmom," or just to go there alone to meditate and nap. She was a Catholic girl, like her "Grandmom," and enjoyed the solitude and the company of the treasured statues, Our Lord's picture, and the many books.

Katie enhanced the lives of all in our home and added love and fun. There was no one who could have cherished her puppy companion more than Jessica. They were inseparable, except when Jessica was at school or work, but once home, all life was spent together.

The highlight of each of Katie's six years was her vacation in New Hampshire. Into the family van she would leap and snuggle down next to her "Mother" on one of the large seats, in preparation for the long, 400-mile trip. Jessica had to keep reclaiming her portion of their seat, as Katie would sprawl out more and more with each passing hour. Never causing any trouble, she quietly passed the time in sleep or in viewing sights from the window. As the van pulled into the woods and drove the mile-long dirt road, heading down the private hill to our property by the lake, Katie would leap out as the door slipped open and set her four feet on "Higher Ground," as we called this special place. All felt exhilarated at journey's end, despite the long trip, for this place of peace truly is a touch of heaven. Surrounded by all of God's creations—trees, rocks, water, and sky above—the name of the property, taken from an old hymn, aptly applies—for one surely has the experience of a higher and richer sort of living when on Higher Ground. Katie knew this too. She felt the utter freedom of running about the woods near the cottage and dashing into the lake whenever she pleased. She had no worries here. She filled her daytime hours with play and her evenings with watching the family members read or play games. When drowsiness took over, she would curl up and slumber in a corner until bedtime. Then off she would go upstairs with her "Mother." These were golden days to the golden Katie.

In the last eleven days of her life, Katie had been rewarded with an unexpected vacation and had spent seven and a half of those last days in New Hampshire. It was truly the place she loved most on this earth.

Once home, however, a tragedy descended on the third day. It was mid-evening. While visiting relatives, Katie had been permitted to go outside in the yard briefly by Michael, Jessica's husband. At the moment the front door was opened, not only Katie slipped through but also her "cousin" Bear—a very, very large, dark dog. Unwisely, after playfully perusing the yard, she followed this large companion into unknown areas as they chased each other around and about. Suddenly, without warning, a blue truck bore down upon Katie as she set foot into the forbidden street. With no chance to retract her steps to the safety of the curb, the truck struck her down and sped away.

People came from out of the darkness and assembled about her, with tearful attempts to see if this sweet dog could be saved. But she was gone. Michael appeared, after repeated calls to her to return home. Shaken and devastated, he carried Katie in his arms to his car and laid her inside the trunk.

Jessica, not knowing of the tragedy, remained within the house. Once told and utterly broken in grief, she stood with her husband at the car, and together they recited the Lord's Prayer for their fallen companion. Katie had been Jessica's "daughter" for six and a half years.

Our entire family was shaken by this senseless end to her beautiful life, which should have had so many joyful years still to be lived. Sadness filled the hearts of all those who loved her, and acceptance of her death was refused. Anger too was felt—and no words existed that could remove the pain. Only the best was desired for her earthly body, which once had been a loving presence to us all. Barely able to think or review the events of that dark night, the thought suddenly came to Jessica that there was only one place for Katie to be, and that was in New Hampshire. By no coincidence, for in God there are no coincidences, Bob and I were getting the van ready to leave for the long, nine-hour trip, when the news of Katie's death came. Our plans had been to drive there the previous night, but Our Lord had detained us and opened up, instead, a few lovely hours for us to spend with our daughter Barbara and husband Frank, before leaving for two weeks. So we had postponed our trip for one day, in order to be with these two, whom we loved. By this postponement, we made it possible for Katie to be taken again to the place that she most loved on earth.

Lovingly and tenderly wrapped in a beautiful quilt by Jessica, Katie's body was placed in a large box. Before wrapping the quilt securely around her, Jessica stayed with her quietly alone, grieving for her precious "little girl." Tucking a favorite scarf in with her and removing her collar to keep always as a treasure, Jessica added two daffodils. Broken-hearted, she kissed her little dog for the last time and covered her well.

Michael, Jessica's husband of two years, and George, her brother, brought the coffin carefully to the van and placed it inside about midnight. In the early hours of morning, while still dark, we made the sad, never-to-be-forgotten journey with the adorable Katie, taking her back from whence she had come only three days earlier. What a privilege and an honor to be entrusted with her earthly body. In our grief this became our strength, the caring for this dear dog and friend. For the first time in her young life, Katie did not leap from the van in joy. She remained asleep, in God.

On a brilliant, sunny, cold Sunday, Katie's "Grandpop" dug her grave, ten feet from the lake in which she loved to play and dash about. Her "Grandmom" prepared a Rosary, Crucifix, a love gift of her own bracelet, and a tiny toy belonging to her "cousin" Rochester, and, placing them in a plastic container and marking it within on paper with Katie's full name and dates, Bob securely fastened the box to the coffin.

Katie was laid to rest in her most favorite earth. Rocks she once bounded over were now mounded over her entire grave site to protect and beautify it. Silk flowers were arranged between two of the rocks; then I blessed her grave with Holy Water and prayed. At a prearranged time, Jessica and Michael joined in spirit with us as we stood by the grave on that Sunday evening, holding a loving service for Katie and praying all the prayers that meant so much in their lives. Dear little Katherine Elizabeth, laid to rest on Higher Ground. Always her grave will be a tangible evidence of a beautiful life that brought blessings to each family member. Now on even *"Higher Ground"* than her beloved property in New Hampshire, she romps and plays with Our Lord, carrying all those who loved her and whom she loved, in her heart, forever.

Within the stillness of Higher Ground and deep within my soul I have heard:

"Well done thy good and faithful servant
—Katherine Elizabeth Kolb Drakely.
Welcome Home!"

There is nothing I can say further to tell you of my grief, but Katie's death catapulted me into exploring other areas in relation to animals and humans—particularly to animals and Christians. Also, Rochester's presence in my life, coming as an unexpected gift while Katie was still alive, has only deepened the resolve to delve into the relationship of Christians and animals and to re-evaluate my own life and to make drastic changes in it. These events impressed on me the importance to examine, question, and consider attitudes and conditions that exist among our culture that simply seem a contradiction, if we are claiming to follow the Christian path of love.

Katie & Jessica

PART TWO

❧

*Practicing Nonviolence
and Compassion Towards
All God's Creation*

Rochester looking over the manuscript

CHAPTER NINE

❦

A Call to Abandon the Ostrich Syndrome

"How many a man has dated a new era in his life from reading a book."
—Henry David Thoreau

I WOULD LIKE NOW TO SHARE the deepest of my concerns regarding attitudes and conditions regarding animals, and have you examine them too, perhaps for the first time. Or perhaps similar concerns have struck at your hearts before and continue to do so, but you were not convicted sufficiently enough in your spirit to act, or change, or even discuss these concerns with others. Perhaps in these pages we can privately consider these matters of the human-animal relationship—and seeing them actually written in black and white might cause your heart to move, even melt, in a way that will also bring about a change in the way you view our fellow living beings and also your actions concerning them.

I cannot offer you endless statistics in these matters or delve thoroughly into history involving Christians and their outlook on and involvement with animals. Such writings have already been completed by people far more educated and trained and capable than myself, and there is no reason ever to try to compete with such books. I can only share with you through my own personal experiences and all the while continually point you to other books already written, and pray that the combination of the two will cause you to confront these issues within yourself. Most important, and particularly, I hope the combined impact touches your hearts in a way that will inspire you to take a personal stand as a friend and protector of our fellow beings on earth—the animals. If each one who reads this becomes moved to do something in their own way to relieve the plight of animals, then, along with deep prayer, there can be a new compassion arise from the Christian world to save them. As you read what I am attempting to write, I recommend you also obtain copies of at least two additional books, either through purchasing them or through a friend who owns them, or perhaps from a library.

The first is known as "The Animal Rights Bible," and the first edition appeared in 1975, changing many lives. The new edition I learned about through a review in the *Boston Globe*, which was accompanied by a picture of the author. It was given high acclaim, and I ordered it through a local New Hampshire bookstore, to be my companion in the months while I wrote this book. I can read only a few pages of it at a time, because the tragic information it reveals makes me cry. I have to put it aside until I feel stronger emotionally to read and learn more. I recommend this book highly to you—and as Christians and human beings, you cannot refuse to open it and be confronted by the horrendous tragedies that exist and that are committed regularly. The name of the book is *Animal Liberation,* and the author is Peter Singer, an Australian philosopher, teacher, and director of the Centre for Human Bioethics at Monash University, Melbourne. He has taught at University College, Oxford, and in various universities in the United States. He is believed to be responsible for the modern animal rights movement, dating from the 1975 publication of the first edition of *Animal Liberation*. He is President of the Animal Liberation Movement in Victoria and Vice President of the Australian and New Zealand Animal Societies. The price of the second edition in hardback is $19.95, and recently it has come out in paperback for $9.95. It is a New York Review Book distributed by Random House, Inc.

If you are not willing to have your life changed, then do not purchase it or read it. It is only for the brave of heart and those who mean to truly do all that a Christian can do to help with the plight of the animals.

The second book I recommend is an excellent volume of quotations by men and women from all walks of life, famous and not so famous, both living and dead, and of all religions. It is *The Extended Circle—A Commonplace Book of Animal Rights,* edited by Jon Wynne-Tyson and published by Paragon House, New York. This thick paperback ($12.95) I also obtained by ordering through our local New Hampshire bookstore. I read from this book daily, and it too brings tears. Some quotations I cannot bear to read over, having once digested them—but seeing there the person's name who stated each thought is enough to remind me of all it contains. This book cannot ever be set aside, once this new conviction regarding animals is put into your heart by Our Lord. The reading of it is a constant spur that we cannot go on as we are.

I pray you will obtain these two books in some way, either now as you continue to read further along in this small volume, or after you have completed it. Though either book is powerful alone, it is better to obtain both, since they are different in nature and content. They truly complement each other and are essentials to the Christian home and reader.

Three additional books, each priced at $4.95, made their appearance in bookstores in the fall of 1990. That three new ones should appear then (and many more since) indicates the need and interest in this subject. These also are excellent, and I gave copies of each to all my children and to the families of the married ones for Christmas. I pray that parents will read them to children too young to read, to instill love of animals, and that the children who can read will spend time on their own with them. I have also given copies to many friends and to my priest (only one of these three titles to each—buying equal amounts of each). They are affordable and filled with information to help you help the animals. The titles are:

- 🐾 *67 Ways to Save the Animals,* by Anna Sequora with Animal Rights International.
- 🐾 *Save the Animals,* by Ingrid Newkirk, National Director, PETA (People for the Ethical Treatment of Animals)
- 🐾 *The Animal Rights Handbook: Everyday Ways to Save Animal Lives.* This is book is a combined effort of many people.

These three are recommended for your use in addition to the first two—NOT to replace them. Now let us move on, as I share some of the things I have experienced or known of, along with conversations and scenes I have witnessed, both good and bad, that have helped bring me to where I am, aside from having Rochester move into our hearts and home and change our lives.

In loving memory of

Inky (Gray)
My childhood black cat

Mitzi (Gray)
My childhood cat after Inky

Lizzie (Kolb)
A little brown,
Cairn Terrier

CHAPTER TEN

❧

A Challenge to Christians: Do Unto Others

"There is no religion without love, and people may talk as much as they like about their religion, but if it does not teach them to be good and kind to other animals as well as humans, it is all a sham."
—Anna Sewell (*Black Beauty*)

SINCE ROCHESTER'S COMING INTO MY LIFE, my life has changed so drastically that I see this world and humans in a new way. I can no longer live in the same manner as in the past with regard to animals. Though I have always had a love for animals, my eyes were not opened to things as I see them now, until I experienced this deeper relationship with Rochester. It did not take long, either, before that change came to be, and every day it becomes more ingrained in me, so that I could never ever be as I was before.

I want to relate some startling incidents—at least they were startling to me—that involved Christians in regard to animals. I cannot accept them as being morally right, but I place them here for you to consider with regard to what your own actions might be in similar circumstances.

A Christian woman of our acquaintance, one of the finest we know, who would do anything to help another human being and who is known

45

for having a heart of gold in this respect, was driving along a country road in Pennsylvania. The back of the truck was loaded with odds and ends she planned to get rid of, but they were not really packed in well. Suddenly she saw a small cat ahead, headed for the middle of the road. To avoid hitting it, she began to drive in a weaving manner as she approached it, for no one was behind her. Nonetheless, the little cat was running in the road in such a way that her wheels could not avoid him. Her choice at that point was not to stop, fearing that the top portion of the load she was carrying in the truck might fall out and spill all over the road. And so she proceeded ahead, hit the little cat, and killed it! Although she was a devout Christian, the inconvenience of losing her load was more important than the life of the cat. She felt sorry for the cat, but thought she had done the right thing.

A man, while driving on a quiet suburban road, was observing things in the rearview mirror when he suddenly struck a dog who ran into his path. He saw it, felt the impact, and left the scene.

After he left the scene, his only concern was that he may have been seen—not concern for the life of the dog. Finally, to confirm in his own mind that he had not been seen, he anonymously called the police so they might check this area. He took no responsibility, confessed nothing, and offered no help to the animal or to the family the animal belonged to, if it should have had one. The police at this point knew nothing about what had transpired. Unfortunately, this man was a "Christian" pastor, whom others look up to as a model in Christian living.

A Christian woman who prides herself on her strictness in her Christian life, one who has remained in the limelight and feels she is a model to others, picked up a tiny china lamb from a creche scene on her table that a grandchild was enamored by. She sweetly began to show the child the "dear little lamb" and tell that Jesus was called the Lamb of God. She explained how He cared for all the little lambs and how we must be kind to animals. Much fuss over the little china lamb—yet only ten minutes earlier she had finished eating a lamb dinner in the presence of this same child. I leave you to consider this paradox. Mahatma Gandhi has said in *An Autobiography: The Story of My Experiments*:

To my mind, the life of the lamb is no less precious than that of a human being. I should be unwilling to take the life of the lamb for the sake of the human body. I hold that the more helpless a creature, the more entitled it is to protection by man from the cruelty of man.

Some devout Christians cannot seem to comprehend that an animal can be a fit and loving companion, and in some cases a person's only companion, and that it can be a fulfilling relationship for the human who loves his or her companion so. I have seen shock, disdain, and disbelief when prayer is mentioned or given for an animal—and the disdain comes from Christians who have reputations for deep prayer lives. Why are Christians different from those of other faiths and religions in this way? And how can it continue if we expect to be witnesses to the world? I have heard Christians say, "I hate animals," and then laugh and think it is amusing.

I have tears within and feel deeply troubled when, from the altars of churches, pastors and priests announce a ham-and-bean dinner for their parishioners, to be served in the church halls. It saddens me that Christians after attending Mass and feeding upon the Eucharist, Our Lord's Body and Blood, would then go with their pastor and feed on the dead bodies of many pigs. These many pigs had to be slaughtered in order for this large group to have an evening of sociability and fun, when the same fellowship could be achieved without the suffering and slaughter of those animals. If one would but read about pigs and learn of their intelligence and what they endure and suffer before the actual horrendous slaughter itself, then one could never eat a pig again.

Naturalist W.H. Hudson, in *Book of a Naturalist* (as quoted in John Robbins' *Diet for a New America*), has said:

I have a friendly feeling towards pigs and consider them the most intelligent of beasts. . . . I also like his attitudes towards all other creatures, especially man. He views us from a totally different, a sort of democratic standpoint, as fellow citizens and brothers, and takes for granted, or grunted, that we understand his language, and without servility or insolence, he has a natural, pleasant, camaraderie—or hail-fellow-well-met air with us.

My husband, whose soul has been enlightened concerning animals and who eats now in a different way, even slows down and brakes for the tiny chipmunks that run into country roads. This happens spontaneously, and it gives us such joy to know that little lives are spared. He never intentionally harmed animals before, but now he is even more aware and seeks to be especially cautious.

J. Todd Ferrier (1855-1943), in *On Behalf of Creatures*, states:

> *Western civilization, in seeking to conquer the east, has too often materialized the faith. And the failure of missionaries to win over the cultured of the east is through our gross western habits in living. For the man whose religion teaches him to hold all life sacred is not likely to be converted to a faith that deems no life sacred but man's.*

Ferrier continues, in *The Extended Circle: A Commonplace Book of Animal Rights*, to say:

> *Much of the indifference, apathy, and even cruelty which we see, has its origin in the false education given the young concerning the rights of animals and their duty towards them. . . . It ought to make all who profess evangelical Christianity ashamed, that the finest and most compassionate souls have not been within their own borders, but rather amongst those whose deepest thoughts have aroused the suspicion of heresy. Evangelical Christianity, as people understand it, has absolutely failed to kindle the Divine Compassion, and to realize itself in a great fire of sacred devotion to all life.*

In loving memory of our three cairn terriers, left to right:
Crackers, Muffin, and Lizzie

CHAPTER ELEVEN

❖

Stories of Christian Compassion for All Creatures

*"This god-like sympathy grows and thrives and spreads far beyond
the teaching of churches and schools where too often the mean, blinding,
loveless doctrine is taught that animals have neither mind, nor soul,
have no rights that we are bound to respect, and were made only
for man, to be petted, spoiled, slaughtered or enslaved.*
—John Muir, *The Story of My Boyhood*

TODAY THE MANY CHRISTIANS who do have compassion for all life and who are deeply concerned about the animals that share the earth with us are not a majority and therefore are often argued with or scorned by shaking heads—incredulous that it could be considered wrong to slaughter and eat other living creatures. I have experienced these judgments strongly from other Christians and even our close friends. It is very difficult to be a Christian who does not conform in these ways, especially when others claim Jesus fished and ate meat and that there is no substantial evidence in scripture to say otherwise. As a Christian, I do not have all the answers, but I believe that the Holy Spirit continues to speak to individual hearts in each generation, giving new illumination on spiritual matters and insights into the Holy Word, the Bible. I believe the Holy Spirit motivates us and convicts us of matters in our personal lives and of concerns in the world, and I believe He raises up leaders and followers to make the world a better place to live for all. If this cannot include the animals also—that their world too that they share with us cannot become a better, kinder place to be—then this causes great questions in my soul and mind. I cannot believe that the compassion and mercy of Our Lord does not extend to the animal world, which He created along with humans and all else in His creation. Albert Schweitzer has written about man:

> *Until he extends the circle of his compassion to all living things, man will not himself find peace.*

This quotation inspired the title of the book referred to above, *The Extended Circle*. We have seen pictures since childhood of Our Lord surrounded by little children and animals, often with words of scripture accompanying those pictures: *"Let the little ones come unto Me."* Would He truly endorse the killing of such animals under cruel circumstances, for food, for science—or not care? He was born in a stable amongst the gentle beasts and animals. They were His first companions, aside from His Parents. Has He no special love and concern for those He first saw with baby eyes?

The answer must be "yes," for Jesus taught us the Golden Rule: *"Do unto others as you would have them do unto you."*

Many Christians do sincerely care about God's own creatures and do reach out to help them in numerous ways. Some of those stories, personally known to me, are included here. Christians are often involved in Humane Societies and Animal Rescues and are Animal Rights Activists. I am so thankful for these people, as well as for the non-Christians involved, who are giving of themselves to do all they can to stop slaughter, hunting, vivisection, experimentation, and the killing of dolphins, whales, seals, and elephants. Their desire to help animals causes them to give up other things in their lives in order to help these suffering animals, fish, birds, and every creature possible. I cannot tell you in detail about those who are not of my personal acquaintance; I can speak to you only out of my own personal experience, and that I do not see a great love of animals or deep concern for them in the Christian religion, at large, except in the isolated situations that I relate here.

Perhaps the Holy Spirit has impressed on me to write about these concerns, because apathy, uncaring, and even total disregard for animals in general can be seen and felt among the Christian community.

A Little Squirrel

I read an account recently about a man who was driving down a country road, when a squirrel darted out unexpectedly in front of him. He tried in vain to avoid hitting the squirrel, but he simply could not avoid it. The man was crushed and overwhelmed at what he had done and did not think such a thing could affect him so deeply. He picked up the limp body of the little squirrel so that no other vehicle could run over it, and he took it to a densely wooded area, after walking some distance. He placed the little body in some leaves at the base of a tree, then covered the body with additional leaves. Finding he had tears, he was struck deeply that he had killed. He said the first things that came to mind were things his mother had taught him in childhood about saying he was sorry if he had done something wrong and then saying prayers to Our Lord. And so, there beneath the big tree by the body of the little squirrel, he told Our Lord he was sorry that he had caused the death—though unintentionally—and then he said prayers for the little squirrel, including "Now I Lay Me Down to Sleep."

He said it was as if all the rightness his mother had taught him as a boy suddenly surfaced and became the means by which he laid the small squirrel to rest in a fitting Christian way. Still deeply saddened by what he had done, he left at last. He said it was an experience he will always remember, and it taught him anew the sanctity of all life when he saw that he had taken a life. He felt that the prayers and memories that surfaced instantly of childhood were meant to remind him that Our Lord loves all living creatures.

This account made me cry and gave me such hope. I will never forget this happening either, and the sensitivity of this grown man over the death of the small squirrel. What a wonderful world this would be if all humans were as this man. I am certain this incident affected the man in other areas of his life as he went his way. After showing such compassion for such a tiny one, one can only imagine how much more compassion he continues to give

Ralph, the Compassionate Squirrel

Another story concerning a squirrel was so moving that I knew I must share it in this book. A friend, Marie, is a woman of compassion who has fed homeless cats for years and ministered to them when wounded. She wrote me about a little gray tabby cat that she and her husband gave to their five-year-old son for Christmas. The cat became a member of the family. At age twelve, the cat was injured, and the veterinarian said he would never walk again. It was summer, and the saddened boy and his parents made a comfortable little box for the cat and would take him outdoors with them. Someone was always with him as he rested in his little box. He was a mild little cat and had never tried to hurt the birds and squirrels that Marie regularly fed. Among those was a sassy little squirrel the family had nicknamed "Ralph," who always ate the birdseed. Marie would gently scold him but eventually bought him his own peanuts. The squirrel became very tame and would come running if they called his name. He often hopped onto the picnic table and patted the family members who were there, to remind them to give him his peanuts. He would then gently eat them from the hand that held them out to him.

When the family brought out the little injured cat in the box, Ralph came over to investigate and realized the cat was sick. He returned to his own peanuts, took a peanut, and went over to the cat, and laid the peanut in the box beside him. Marie wrote that it was as if Ralph was saying, *"I'll feed you. I know you are sick."* From then on, he always looked in on the cat. Contrary to the veterinarian's opinion, the little cat did walk again, though not in the same way as before he was injured.

This true story struck me so, and it brought to mind a quotation that I have used elsewhere in this book. Meister Eckhart said:

> *All creatures desire to speak God in their works: they all speak Him as well as they can, but they cannot really pronounce Him.*

Most certainly this little squirrel Ralph was "speaking God" in his works, as well as he could. His ministering to the little cat with his own peanuts was truly a form of prayer in the creature world, and in the human world also. Our work and our deeds are forms of prayer, and little

Ralph was "praying his friend well" with each peanut and visit. His prayer joined with the loving prayers of the cat's family—and the cat walked again.

If we would just take time to really see and to watch creatures more frequently, I believe we would have many amazing tales to share with each other.

Many Christians in this world—and non-Christians as well—not only have compassion for an injured animal or creature, but also actually do something about it. My own daughter Barbara and son-in-law Francis are examples of this spirit, for they tenderly care for animals and their needs whenever a need presents itself. They have had many experiences with animals, once even spending close to $200.00 to have a veterinarian's care for a week for a little kitten that had crawled onto their porch, so badly injured that he would have died, had they not intervened.

Here is another incident related to me by Francis.

Guest from Above

Francis' workshop is in a small building situated on the rear of their property, some distance from their old, stone, three-story home. One summer day in August, he was busy in his workshop, when he suddenly became aware of a strange noise outside the open door. Leaving his work, he went to the door and immediately discovered the source of the sound.

On the ground was a pigeon, thrashing about wildly and obviously injured. Francis was struck with sympathy for the bird and picked him up. The bird continued to thrash and jerk and move his whole being erratically as he lay in the palms of Francis' hands.

The pigeon's suffering struck Francis' heart, and he placed the bird in one hand and covered him with the palm of the other. The warmth and gentle pressure of this loving embrace brought a calm to the injured one. The thrashing stopped, and a peace seemed to come to the little bird. He lay quietly, wrapped in the blanket of Francis' large hands. This gave Francis peace also.

He entered his workshop with his little patient and found a proper-size box. He placed soft clothes in the box and then gently lay the pigeon in his new bed. The bird again began to jerk violently and behave as before—and so the man lightly covered him with the extra cloth, to allow the bird again to feel comfort and protection.

He carried the little patient in his box bed to the rear of his workshop and placed it on a shelf quite hidden and high. Because he and Barbara had two cats that he had taken in and given a fine home, he put the little bird in this hidden place so the cats would not discover it.

Leaving the shop and his new charge, Francis looked about to see what might have caused the bird to be injured. At once he noticed the electrical wires just above where the bird had fallen on his driveway. He reasoned that his little friend had hit the wires while in flight and perhaps broken its neck. This would explain the violent motions and continuous jerking of the body.

He could think of nothing more to do at the moment except tell Barbara, his wife. Just several weeks before they had found a tiny injured bird smaller than the pigeon and had brought him into their home and given him a bed also, and nourishment. Upon his gradual recovery, they had placed him outdoors and found he had truly grown strong. He flew away. But this one, the pigeon, was different and very ill.

Francis went into their home and brought Barbara outdoors to the workshop, all the while telling her the details surrounding his discovery and care of the bird. Barbara, a registered nurse, shared his concerns for little creatures and animals.

When they arrived at the little patient's bed upon the shelf, they could hear and see him still moving about, due to his severe injury. Barbara felt great pity too, for there seemed little they could do to comfort him further.

Gently Francis reached in and picked up the bird in his strong hand and again covered the shaking body with his other hand, as he had done before, in a gentle but firm embrace. Once more the pigeon grew calm and quiet. There was a special silence that descended upon the trio.

Suddenly the bird lifted its little head, and with its dark, beady little eyes fixed upon his friend and physician, he stared right into Francis' eyes and down to the depths of his soul. Then his little head collapsed backwards and he died.

Francis knew in that instant of deep communion with the bird that it indeed was a moment that transcended both time and place. Deep within, he knew from the look in the bird's eyes that his little patient was saying "thank you," and that the bird had patiently survived and waited for the man's return, so that he could wordlessly communicate his gratitude deeply to the heart of his friend. Only then, did the pigeon give up his life.

In that one searching look from the bird's eyes, Francis had felt God. And Francis surely follows the great model, St. Francis of Assisi, in the love and caring for all living creatures. In the words of Jesus, the Great Healer, *"If you have done it unto the least of these, you have done it unto Me."* Surely this fallen one was "one of the least."

As Francis and Barbara buried their feathered friend, they knew they had been touched by God through the bird's brief intrusion in their lives. Those dark beady eyes marked with gratitude will forever leave a Holy imprint upon the soul of Francis.

To me it is obvious that Our Lord truly speaks to us through His beloved creatures, and therefore, for me, it is impossible to ever do harm to any one of them. Abraham Lincoln replied to friends who chided him for delaying them when he stopped to return a fledgling to its nest, *"I could not have slept tonight if I had left that helpless little creature to perish on the ground."* Though we may not directly harm a creature ourselves, by not helping one in trouble, we are indirectly adding to its plight. Lincoln also said, *"I am in favor of animal rights as well as human rights. That is the way of a whole human being."* He also spoke out and declared, *"I care not much for a man's religion whose dog and cat are not the better for it."* I find his words maxims that can inspire myself and many to higher living in this world.

Homes for Lost Cats

I know a wonderful young woman, Norma, who has a special mission in caring for and reaching out to lost and homeless cats. For years she cared for two beloved cats of her own, "Hobbit" and "Sneakers." Recently, after a long illness, Sneakers died. He died in her arms as she was cradling him, and with his little paw he reached up and touched her face in great love as he left her. Her heart was crushed, just as it would be for any beloved human companion. This little cat had been with her constantly for many years and cared for and talked to and treated with love and respect. I understood her heartbreak and grief. Many do.

Norma continues to help and feed cats that she finds or who come to her door, and she goes a step further by placing notices everywhere, telling of the cat and its complete description. If no one claims the cat after a long period, then she tries to find a good home for the cat. Often I receive calls from Norma to tell me of the latest little one she is caring for and to ask my help in trying to find the perfect person who would love and care for it. She does not give up. Once a home is found, then she personally has the cat neutered or spayed before giving him to his new owner, and she pays for this as well as a check-up. The person taking the cat home is told that if he is not happy with his new companion, he is to return him to Norma and not turn him out again. She wants the safety of the cat assured, and she is willing to again try to find a new home. I learned of Norma's love through her aunt, Ruth, a close friend of mine; then I met her when I went with my daughter to Norma's home when there was a beautiful little cat waiting there for someone to care for her. My daughter June brought the cat home, and Daisy has since been a part of June's family. I am thankful for loving people like Norma—and June. June has always loved animals and was a true friend to our three little Cairn Terriers while she was growing up. Now June has, in addition to Daisy, a beloved Collie, "Molly," and Molly and June have been close companions for over eight years. Though June and Rob have six children, one can see by Molly's actions that she belongs truly to June.

A Christian friend of mine, Charlotte, also feeds all the lonesome cats of her neighborhood as well as her own two lovely ones, "Ranger" and "Chester." She too, like Francis and Barbara, has paid for extensive treatment for an injured cat, one she could not keep but one who was made whole and well and ready for adoption. "Her boys," as she calls her cats, are always well fed and cared for, no matter what other problems may be present in her life. They are her beloved companions, and she has since added a dog to her family.

Gina, another Christian friend, cares for stray animals while caring for her own cat Luanne and dog DawnAlice. For months she has provided food and a sleeping bag to nestle into, to a lost cat whose owner she has been unsuccessful in locating.

Concern for a Chained Dog

My daughter Laurel is troubled about a neighbor's dog that is chained continuously to a dog house with only a few feet of chain. The dog has lived her entire life in that condition and gone through pregnancy after pregnancy. The dog is a captive prisoner and available for any male dog that is interested. Litter after litter is born to this little dog, sometimes in the freezing cold, and the dogs all remain outdoors or in the dog house, only a few yards from a busy street. Laurel constantly watches out for the puppies so they will not get lost or harmed until the owner again finds homes for them. Laurel has called authorities about the situation, but nothing can be done, because a dog house has been provided. However, it is not insulated, and the dog has spent her life chained to it. We can only pray at some point in the future that this dog's life can be saved and that she can live in a higher way. I am grateful that Laurel does all that she can in this situation.

The Cat by the Side of the Road

Another incident concerns a Christian woman who helped a poor little cat here in New Hampshire. Three summers ago a cat was struck by a car on the road in our little town and the driver fled the scene. I could not bear to see the little animal there in the road, injured, with no assistance, for he was in danger of being crushed by another car. I stopped at the side of the road and got out and stood with the cat. He was terribly injured, and I felt so sad. Within minutes, another car stopped and a woman joined me. We knew the cat might not let us touch him, and so it was decided that she would get help from a nearby garage attendant who cared about animals, while I kept my post with the cat to protect him. As I knelt in the road and talked softly to the little animal, I felt I had calmed him. I prayed and soothed him, and my heart broke as I observed his injuries and bleeding that was obvious. As I looked into his eyes and he into mine, I knew without a doubt he was no different than I was. He was one of God's creatures, he was suffering, and I felt I had been drawn into another realm as this dear little cat and I held each other fast with our eyes and I soothed him with prayers. We paid no heed to the cars that had to detour to get around us. To this day I see that cat's sweet face and feel his eyes when I quietly reflect on those moments. I truly felt like I had been allowed to share in a new spiritual exchange between human and creature.

The woman returned with the young man, and he, too, was visibly concerned and upset over the cat's condition. His plan was to gently lift him and take him immediately to a veterinarian. But as the man approached the cat, with a sudden, almost supernatural burst of energy, the cat leaped past me from the road and into the underbrush, leaving a pool of blood and urine. As I had caressed and held him with prayers and my eyes, he had urinated to such a degree as he lay there that I felt perhaps it was a sign that his organs had been injured or an indication that he was dying. We searched but could not find him, and this saddened the three of us further. The other woman and myself left eventually, trusting the young man, who said that if he could possibly find him, he would take him for medical attention. Though I looked for the kind man often, I never saw him again. It was as if he were an angel who appeared and then disappeared—there only to give us confidence concerning the little cat. I will never forget that little cat and all that transpired. I cannot tell you if the woman and young man were Christians, but they gave of themselves to aid an injured animal, no matter what their religion.

The Ultimate Home for Stray Cats

A Christian couple we know, Joe and Connie, have taken care of stray cats in ways that show the ultimate in compassion. Joe has built homes out of cardboard and covered them with plastic and placed carpets and heaters in them. Similar homes are in the garage. Some of these same strays have lived in these homes for thirteen to fourteen years; others come and then leave. Many births have happened, and they tend to all the needs of these cats. At one point they had eight indoor cats. Recently Connie's beloved cat, who lived indoors all his life and shared life with Connie, died suddenly of cancer. Her heart was truly broken. My heart was moved deeply also as first we prayed for Tiger's recovery and then through sharing Connie's grief when his death came. A death of a beloved and constant friend is crushing and deep.

Ginny

My close friend Ginny is truly devoted to animals, not only her own beloved ones but also those of others. Numerous times she has been on a highway driving and seen a stray dog. She has taken the risk of stopping and befriending the dog each time, in order to get it into her car so that she might read its tags. In all cases, she has driven around until she has found the dog's home and owner. In each instance, she was treated with appreciation. In one case, the owner believed his dog to be in his back yard and was in disbelief to see the dog with Ginny. Ginny has fervently prayed for animals (her own and mine and others), and it was she who helped me the night Katie was struck by the truck. Though it was late, she continued to call me periodically until well after midnight and she knew all arrangements had been made for Katie's trip and burial in New Hampshire—and that she had done all she could to help me remain calm. She would have been willing to drive up from New Jersey to Pennsylvania at that late hour if I had needed her with me, but I felt she had given all that she could through her loving and numerous calls.

Darrell Sifford and B.G.

A wonderful, sensitive columnist for the *Philadelphia Inquirer*, Darrell Sifford, whose recent death by drowning affected deeply all who read his columns, wrote about the death of his eleven-year-old cat, B.G. He said he felt a sense of loss, *"a loss of such depth that I'm not sure it could be comprehended by anybody who has not really loved a pet, invited it into family membership, and given it the rights and responsibilities that accompany membership."* The response to that column began immediately, and he received sympathy cards, letters, poems, and even flowers from people who had also lost pets and who recalled how the terrible sting of sorrow had remained for so very long. Some people did not understand, and he also received nasty, fresh letters—but oh, the other responses were so dear to him. Many wrote of their sorrow, too, and he included four or five of these letters. He showed compassion to the people who were also in sorrow by letting them share their grief with him and the readers. Darrell's writings and sensitivity brought tears to my eyes—and the other letters also. Darrell related how each morning upon awakening, when his little cat B.G. was right there with him, he would say, *"B.G., can you understand how very much I love you?"* This made me teary also, because I say similar things to Rochester every day and night. Then, after B.G. died, Darrell would visit his grave regularly and say, *"B.G., can you understand how very much I miss you?"* Now, less than a year later, Darrell and B.G. are together again. The world was a better place because of this fine loving columnist, and surely Darrell felt this was true also because of the gift of B.G. in his life.

"The Guardian Angel"

I have met a new Christian friend in New Hampshire, a young woman who is a church organist, elementary school teacher, and a caregiver to animals. She is a model to her students as a protector of animals and of the vegetarian way of life. Through examples, she has been able to share the plight of many of God's creatures, even to having each student experience being confined in a small crate, as veal calves must for their entire short lives. One student built a crate such as this, and each child got down on all fours and one at a time got an inkling of what it would be like to live in that cramped space and never to live on the outside. This teacher knows some converts to vegetarianism were made that day. In her own home she shares life with two parakeets, two quail, one dog, a tarantula(!), a turtle, and a recovering pigeon—though new creatures are added regularly. She also has cats, three rabbits, and a wild opossum who comes to her porch through the cat door and helps himself to the cat food.

Cindy does not really have room for all these creatures she cares for and loves, but she has confided that she often feels like a "Guardian Angel" is saying to her, *"Take this creature—you will not regret it."*

In speaking with her and in reading her beautiful letter that contained pictures of her own cats and a dear little seal with big eyes peering at me (a lovely drawing at the bottom of her sheet of writing paper), I knew it was *she* who was Guardian Angel to so many little ones of His.

. . . To the Least of These . . .

Rose-Beth, another dear Christian friend is known for her devotion to her own Boston terrier "Buck" and Russian Blue cat "Nora," but she also is kind to the wildlife around her and even puts little pellets on the kitchen countertop each night before sleep, so that her "house mouse" will not go hungry that evening. She is interested in and loving to all creatures she meets.

The Love That Opened Our Home

My son George is another example of Christian love for animals. He wanted to be a veterinarian when he was quite young, and he has always been a friend to animals since he was a small boy. It was his love for them that caused the first smaller pets to come into our home and join our large family—followed by three dogs.

CPR Saves a Kitten

An article sent to me recently by my friend Ruth tells a most beautiful story of a firefighter who, with a team of firefighters, was able to ensure the rescue of a six-member family from a burning mobile home. When that was accomplished, they also saved six kittens. One kitten would not have lived, had this firefighter not done mouth-to-mouth resuscitation, which was the first time he had ever attempted

CPR for a small kitten. He said he just scaled down the CPR to fit the kitten's small size, and the technique was basically the same as for humans.

He said it has been overwhelming—and not in his wildest dreams would he ever have thought this small act would be so well-received. He said that nothing he has done in his twenty-five years of firefighting compares with the attention he has received since performing this act of love. The firefighter and his wife adopted the little kitten following this incident. The other kittens at this time were also up for adoption. Most of the responses spoke of how the firefighters made the effort to save the kittens (and the one in particular who showed no sign of life), because they consider pets as a part of the family. That is what warmed the hearts of the readers of the newspaper upon seeing the picture of the man reviving the kitten.

A Precious Life Cut Short

Our Christian friends Jack and Clara in New Hampshire have fed their neighbor's cat for a very long period and provided other interest and comfort to him. Each day his food is placed in a nice dish within an enclosed vestibule of their home, so he can enjoy his meal in warmth away from rain or winter cold. He was made an outside cat by his uncaring owner, and no sincere thoughts were taken of him. He was a friendly little thing, black and white, and usually outside our friends' home when we would visit. Last year, however, as winter approached, the owner decided she did not want to have him in her basement at all, even though a very cold and snowy season was predicted. One day, Clara called to tell us the little cat had been taken to the veterinarian and euthanized, because the owner was too selfish even to allow him some space in her basement. We felt such sadness over his death—a healthy cat destroyed for the selfish motives of a human. Our friends told us he was deaf and could not hear approaching cars in their rather secluded road, and that was the key reason for the decision. Nevertheless, it saddened me, for he did live where there were both seclusion and very few cars. I can still see him sitting atop our van enjoying the view from this high place while we visited with Jack and Clara. He was sweet and added a loving presence to those who cared. I know in his little heart he was grateful—and loved Jack and Clara. It upset me, too, that he had a very degrading name, and it seemed improper to even use it. How terrible humans can be to animals—putting them so far beneath them in their distorted and unfeeling thinking, giving them undignified and nasty names to point fun, not feeding them, and keeping them outdoors where there is great risk to their lives present in all forms, with no periods of respite at all within the home.

Tires—and Cats

All of this is in complete opposition to the thinking and actions of a fine man in Philadelphia named Guy Giordano, who was written about in an article in the *Philadelphia Inquirer* about one year ago by a staff writer, Beth Gillin. This man likes cats unabashedly, wholeheartedly, and without embarrassment, states this article, and in his South Philadelphia tire shop this mechanic keeps a brood of twenty cats. Pets are not allowed in the condominium that he and his wife share, and so this sixty-one-year-old gentleman keeps his beloved pets in his workshop, where they are fussed over by all who come in. He feels having a pet gives organization to his life and gives him someone to care for and come home to—like a child. He does not have any children.

But he does not just let them live within his workshop; he treats them with deep, loving care. Each one has a dignified name, given for a special reason, and they have quilts to lie on and to snuggle in, teddy bears to cuddle with, and all his cats are treated with love and respect. They have been brought to him by others after being rescued from cruelty or abandonment, or he has found them himself in situations such as these.

All Mr. Giordano's cats are protected by the wearing of name tags on leather collars (blue for boys, pink for girls), and all have their shots up-to-date and have been neutered or spayed.

Each cat seems to have a story associated with it, and one cat he calls his "Rent-A-Cat," because he is picked up each morning at eight by a neighbor who is a writer who likes a companion during the day. Then he is returned in the evening. When Mr. Giordano attends fancy business dinners, he asks the maitre d' to give him all the leftover scraps of meat, and through this his cats have dined on very elegant meals. But he himself buys 150 cans of cat food every two months and 20-lb. bags of dry food (high protein) at a time. To add to their fine treatment, he serves his cats on china plates, which he obtains when a supermarket has a sale. One of the cats' favorite china plates is one given to their owner by former Mayor Frank Rizzo that has Mr. Rizzo's picture featured. The picture, however, is usually covered by a little mound of cat food.

Mr. Giordano truly is a modern day St. Francis of Assisi, and I have had such pleasure from rereading this article often and thinking on the loving attention, care, and protection this man gives daily to dear little defenseless cats that would otherwise have died, usually in a horrible way.

The Holy Blessing

To those animals that have been struck down by passing cars on the roads and highways or killed in other ways, a Methodist Pastor of our acquaintance shows still further compassion to God's creatures. He gives each fallen animal a blessing, making the Sign of the Cross upon them, as he finds them. After doing this loving act for some time, he learned that his wife, also a Christian Pastor, was giving fallen ones this same blessing too.

If I could talk to many individual Christians and question them in depth about their feelings for animals and all creatures God made, and write a very detailed report, I pray that it would be uplifting and cancel out my present inner conviction that there is an overall lack of caring for such as these in the Christian community. I do not intend to take a poll or delve into strangers' lives about these matters. I can, I repeat, only write from my own experience. Because what I do see and hear and experience among Christians, with the exception of these accounts I have related, is not the caring and compassion and love I feel Christians should exhibit and witness to the world, I have felt the need to share all that I have through the writing of this book. May I be proven wrong as time passes.

I pray that all these examples may ignite only the flame of love for animals in every Christian heart and mobilize Christians into becoming informed about animals and animal rights and what they as Christians can do for their fellow creatures with whom they share this world.

I read recently a tender account of an inscription that was found on a small, new gravestone after a devastating air raid on Britain during World War II. Some thought it was a famous quotation, but it was learned that the words were written by a lovely old lady whose pet had been killed by a Nazi bomb. The inscription read, *"There is not enough darkness in all the world to put out the light of one small candle."*

People with beloved animal companions or who have sorrowed over their loss will truly understand this woman's love and grief for her lost companion. This pet had been the light of her life in the darkness of the war. There is darkness in our world today for many reasons, and a very large segment of the darkness is that of the indifference and cruelty toward His creatures. We can make sure that our small candles are kept lit, and we will not be overcome; instead, we will overcome this suffering and these atrocities toward those creatures put into our care.

"NOW WHAT? I TOLD YOU I HAD ASKED MY BEST FRIEND TO BE THE BEST MAN!"

CHAPTER TWELVE

❧

Vegetarianism

"Animals are my friends, and I don't eat my friends."
—George Bernard Shaw

O UR LORD HAS ALWAYS USED BOOKS to lead me along in my spiritual journey. I have been an avid reader since I was a child, and therefore it would seem that He chose the love of reading, which was close to my heart, to draw me more deeply into His Own Heart. Conversions and turning points in my existence were always associated with some book or books, and in reminiscing are naturally connected to these events most firmly. It was not strange then that I was led to make my commitment to vegetarianism through the finding and reading of a book, all within a short period of several days.

But before I write of this in detail, I want to say that since my change and enlightenment through a precious little cat, I often have pain and tears over the things in my past that did not show love to my fellow creatures. I grew up eating meat, poultry, fish, and meals centered around these creatures. I never knew a vegetarian. All my friends grew up in the same way. I am guilty of raising my own family as I was raised, with the usual hamburger, chicken, turkey, occasional roasts, and less seldom, fish. Like millions of Americans and Christians, I made the carcass of a dead animal or bird the centerpiece of a festive meal. I did not know then what I know now. The Holy Spirit simply had not spoken to me about this—or I had not listened.

There was a slight breakthrough in the very early 1980s, when I gave up red meat one Lenten period and never returned to eating it again. But I continued to eat other creatures and serve them to others. Then came macrobiotic cooking lessons in 1983. Our Lord used these cooking lessons to teach me about creatures, and also to learn that nutrition could be sound within a vegetarian lifestyle. He also used the lessons to help me help my husband Bob as he awaited lung surgery in 1984 and to help my Peruvian friend who had cancer. And now I have met many vegetarians. They came to these cooking lessons, some by choice as a preventative, and some because they were trying to heal themselves of cancer, addictions, or other illnesses through this ancient Japanese diet. And I met the teacher and counselors associated with the Macrobiotic Center.

Following these lessons and the using of less and less poultry and no red meat at all in cooking for my family, I began to find it disgusting to see chicken parts or handle them in order to prepare them. Even my two youngest daughters, who often helped me cook, began to experience these same feelings. I no longer could prepare a turkey and found it terrible to see one as the center of attention at Thanksgiving in the home of one of my daughters, who so lovingly had begun to take over my job of having our large family for dinner. But I could never say anything to hurt her, and the first Thanksgiving I was a vegetarian, she did not even know it, for I said nothing. I found myself feeling such guilt each time I ate turkey or chicken (after the macrobiotic cooking lessons) that I rarely ate any, and it had come to be accepted and not particularly noticed one way or the other.

As this past Thanksgiving approached and this matter of the killing of so many turkeys was in the newspaper, I could envision the sadness of this slaughter and the resulting centerpiece at my own approaching family dinner, and I wrote this poem one evening in mild protest and in love for these birds.

WHAT A BEAUTIFUL BIRD?!

O right before our very eyes—
Lies a turkey in demise.

He's there on platter—without head
And all will feed upon the dead.

Now a centerpiece—how odd—
When once he ran about the sod!
All stomachs become graveyards now—
And mashed potatoes bury fowl!

I dedicated it to "All Turkeys." But love of Katie, and then my deep bonding with Rochester, continued to cause the guilt to be unbearable if I did give in, to be polite, and eat poultry. To finally make the spiritual commitment to be a vegetarian was a joy and a relief. It was taken out of my hands from that moment on. I could never go back—the decision was irrevocable! And this decision and commitment has only intensified my love for animals and all creatures of air or water—and also the pain I feel at the inhuman treatment toward them. These feelings will only increase. I just pray that in some way—besides my prayers—that my commitment will be a form of repentance in my life for all the years I was not enlightened, for though I never directly killed an animal, I ate meat, poultry, and fish killed by others. There is no way I can tell you what the animals suffer in order that human beings, millions of them Christians, can have what they feel is a necessity in their diets.

The Animal Rights Maxim is *"Do not eat anything with a face,"* and from that incredible thought and directive, I wrote this little verse one evening:

An excellent rule for the human race—
When sitting down at its dinner place—
To alleviate pain—and death erase
Do not eat anything with a face.

Ralph Waldo Emerson (1803–1882) wrote:

"You have just dined, and however scrupulously the slaughter house is concealed in the graceful distance of miles, there is complicity.

And one can stew it, bake it, broil it, cover it with elegant sauces and fine gravies—but it is still a dead carcass one has prepared and put in the center of the table. In an essay, "On Eating Flesh," an excerpt of which left its impact on my heart from the first reading, the Roman author Plutarch ended by describing the utter torment, torture, and final slow slaughter of animals with these words:

> *. . . for the sake of a little flesh we deprive them of sun, of light, of the duration of life to which they are entitled by birth and being.*

He then delivered this challenge to flesh eaters:

> *If you declare that you are naturally designed for such a diet, then first kill for yourself what you want to eat. Do it, however, only through your own resource, unaided by cleaver or cudgel or any kind of ax.*

The great Renaissance painter, inventor, sculptor, and poet, Leonardo daVinci, said:

> *He who does not value life does not deserve it.*

He considered bodies of meat eaters to be "burial places," graveyards for the animals they eat, and it was his thoughts, read previous to my commitment, that somewhat inspired the poem I wrote. His journals were filled with passages on compassion for animals. He also wrote:

> *Endless numbers of these animals shall have their little children taken from them, ripped open, and barbarously slaughtered.*

A Nonviolent Diet

It has been noted, not only by the famous such as French philosopher Jean-Jacques Rousseau but also in more recent studies by people involved in macrobiotic counselling and cooking, that many meat eaters tend to be more angry and volatile, and that our diets do indeed affect our nature and temperament. "*We are what we eat*" is a well-known saying, and if people would read and study more about how food affects human beings, they would be very surprised at the findings. It is known that women, through their cooking, can make their husbands more relaxed, docile, and laid back. In our own home, there was evidence of this both in my husband's temperament and my own reaction to eating simple brown rice alone for an extended period. There was a definite change in my husband, and any evidence of a short temper disappeared, and he was indeed a happier man. I became so relaxed and content to be absolutely still and contemplative that I had to force myself to do other things. This was an experiment we both tried—living on only short grain brown rice for ten days, as written about in a famous book on the macrobiotic teaching. We later added vegetables and beans and other nourishing ingredients of the macrobiotic diet, but the original ten-day period of eating only short grain organic brown rice was a period of cleansing for the body. It is not harmful—in fact quite the opposite—and monks in Japan and other Eastern countries are known to live exclusively on brown rice. It is the highest food. It truly does make one gentle and compassionate. Yellow-robed Buddhist monks usually go barefoot and carry begging bowls. Besides robe and bowl, a monk owns little else. Other possessions are a needle, a string of 108 beads, which he counts as he meditates on the qualities of Buddha, a razor with which to shave his head, and a filter with which to strain insects from his drinking water so he will do them no harm. If even the insects are protected and cared for, his reverence for life is evident.

Other Vegetarians of Note

So many great men of the past were advocates of natural order and were vegetarians. Pythagoras, famous for contributions to geometry and mathematics, was an example to many who followed thereafter. He ate only herbs, vegetables, and honey, and it was written that he would also pay fishermen to throw their catch back into the sea. Those who followed his teachings were daVinci, Rousseau, Benjamin Franklin, the poet Shelley and his wife, and many others. Benjamin Franklin became a vegetarian at age sixteen and called flesh eating "unprovoked murder" in his autobiographical writings. Unfortunately, many years later he was persuaded to return to the eating of fish.

Russian author Leo Tolstoy advocated "vegetarian pacifism" after a total life change and thereafter never killed anything—not even an ant. He felt that in violence there was a natural progression that culminated in war in human society. He considered flesh eating to be "immoral."

Composer Richard Wagner also believed that all life was sacred. He felt vegetarianism could save mankind from violent tendencies. Henry David Thoreau was a vegetarian at various periods in his life, and though he at times wavered—but returned to the diet—he recognized its virtues. He wrote in *Walden:*

> *Is it not a reproach that man is a carnivorous animal? True, he can and does live in great measure by preying on other animals, but this is a miserable way, as any one who will go to snaring rabbits, or slaughtering lambs, may learn—and he will be regarded as a benefactor of his race who shall reach man to confine himself to a more innocent and wholesome diet. Whatever my own practice may be, I have no doubt that it is a part of the destiny of the human race, in its gradual improvement, to leave off eating animals, as surely as the savage tribes have left off eating each other when they came in contact with the more civilized.*

Mahatma Gandhi is perhaps the one most known for this way of "ahimsa" (or non-violence) and vegetarian diet. He stated:

> *I do feel that spiritual progress does demand at some stage that we should cease to kill our fellow creatures for the satisfaction of our bodily wants.*

He founded Tolstoy Farm, where vegetarian principles were the basis for this community. Gandhi said he did not regard flesh food necessary at any stage and wrote five books on vegetarianism. Gandhi wrote:

> *I hold flesh-food to be unsuited to our species. We err in copying the lower animal world if we are superior to it.*

Gandhi also wrote:

> *The cow is a poem of pity; she is mother to millions of Indian mankind.*

The Hindus see God in everything and in every form: trees and rivers, cows, and even ants. They have reverence for life. This reverence is shown in the principle of "ahimsa." This is why most pious Hindus eat no meat, because it would be against their religion to have an animal killed to provide them with food. Their Scriptures warn, *"All that kill . . . cows, rot in hell for as many years as there are hairs on the body of the (slain) cow."* For a Hindu to eat beef is a sacrilege about equal to cannibalism. The wealthy men endow places to take care of old and decrepit cows, and many Hindus bow deeply to all cows that they pass.

Even insects are protected by "ahimsa." A devout housewife will throw out crumbs as a gift of hospitality to the insects, and on festival days she may put her rice flour before her doorway, having made from it elaborate designs. These designs are good luck symbols that please the spirits who guard the doorway, but they also provide a banquet for the ants.

Throughout all of India's long history her people have depended upon cows and oxen for help. Pulling ploughs and carts, providing milk for drink and food and dung cakes for fuel in the homes, the cow has been India's most valued domestic animal.

In any Indian city, it is startling to see traffic wait patiently while a cow ambles across the street. All are sacred animals, and no loyal Hindu would bring harm to a cow. Their affection for the cow is unique, and the worship of a cow is said to give a married woman sons. It is a worthy religious act to feed any wandering cow.

There are many festivals scattered throughout the year in India, and the animals are given a part in the celebration. Fancy designs are painted on temple elephants, and cows are bathed and their heads decorated in patterns of yellow and red. Hindus believe sacred animals should have a share in happy days. (See *The World's Great Religions*, Life)

Animals are protected in other religions also. In a picture I saw recently of the philosopher LaoTzu, father of Taoism, he is pictured astride an ox. The ox is a symbol of spiritual strength.

Playwright George Bernard Shaw became a vegetarian at age twenty-five, and it was Shelley who opened his eyes to "the savagery of my diet." When people told him that he looked youthful, he said this was not so, that he looked his age. He said it was the other people who looked older than they are, and what could you expect from people who eat corpses? (quoted in *Higher Taste: A Guide to Gourmet Vegetarian Eating*).

Shaw wrote this poem:

> *We pray on Sundays that we may have light*
> *To guide our footsteps on the path we tread;*
> *We are sick of war, we don't want to fight,*
> *And yet we gorge ourselves upon the dead.*

He wrote this as a comment on violence and flesh-eating in human society.

H.G. Wells wrote against the slaughterhouses in "A Modern Utopia," and Nobel-prize winning author Isaac Bashevis Singer became a vegetarian in 1962 at age fifty-eight. He said he was very sorry that he had waited so long, and he finds vegetarianism quite compatible with his mystical variety of Judaism. He made statements I truly appreciate and that are powerful—of how we pray to God for mercy and justice while we continue to eat the flesh of animals that are slaughtered on our account. He states that this is not consistent. The ethical consideration comes first, for him, even though he appreciates the health benefits of vegetarianism. He made this statement:

> *Even if eating flesh was actually shown to be good for you, I would certainly still not eat it.*

Gandhi also believed that ethical principles are the basis for vegetarianism and not reasons of health. I, too, feel as these two men have expressed themselves. Singer became impatient with all the intellectual rationalizing for meat-eating, and he said that various philosophers and religious leaders have tried to convince their disciples and followers that animals are nothing more than machines without a soul, without feelings. But he goes on to state that if anyone who has ever lived with an animal, be it a dog, a bird, or even a mouse, knows that this theory is a brazen lie, invented to justify cruelty. (from *The Higher Taste*)

It is this very point of view that I have been trying to express through the deep sharings concerning my relationship with Rochester.

In the appendix are listed other quotations by Christians concerning non-flesh eating and the vegetarian way, for I have included in this present chapter many thoughts and commitments by non-Christians and from other religions and ways of life.

I have encountered so many statements that touch the soul and cause one to pray and consider the turning away from killing and flesh-eating.

Jean-Jacques Rousseau, mentioned earlier, also wrote this heart-breaking observation that is all truth:

> *The animals you eat are not those who devour others; you do not eat the carnivorous beasts, you take them as your pattern. You only hunger for the sweet and gentle creatures which harm no one, which follow you, serve you, and are devoured by you as the reward of their service.*

Thoreau, whose writings have influenced me for the good in many areas of life, also wrote:

> *No human being past the thoughtless age of boyhood, will wantonly murder any creature which holds its life by the same tenure that he does. (Walden)*

In the same book, he also wrote:

> *I once had a sparrow alight on my shoulder for a moment while I was hoeing in a village garden, and I felt that I was more distinguished by the circumstance than I should have been by any epaulet I could have worn.*

Henry Beston (1888–1968), author of a beautiful book, *The Outermost House*, and a naturalist who once lived on the beach of Cape Cod year round in a little hut, wrote:

> *We need another and a wiser and perhaps a more mystical concept of animals. We patronize them for their incompleteness, for their tragic fate of having taken form so far below ourselves, and therein we err and err greatly. For the animal shall not be measured by man. In a world older and more complete than ours, they move finished and complete, gifted*

with extensions of the senses we have lost or never attained, living by voices we shall never hear. They are not brethren, they are not underlings. They are other nations, caught with ourselves in the net of life and time, fellow prisoners of the splendor and travail of the earth.

And can Christians not be caused to search their souls upon reading these words of other human beings who have answered the call within their souls to respect all life and not kill, torture, and eat creatures that were put on this earth in our trust?

I have been reading for several years on this subject and can come to no other conclusion than I have. I have collected the quotations and thoughts of others in a special Commonplace Book of my own and I will continue to do so. I cannot tell you the sources of all that I have shared with you in this chapter, except that the words came from my own collected ones, and many of these came from *The Extended Circle: A Commonplace Book on Animal Rights*, which I have mentioned earlier, and *The Higher Taste: A Guide to Gourmet Vegetarian Cooking* and *Walden* by Henry David Thoreau.

I will close this chapter with the words once more of Isaac Bashevis Singer (1904–   ):

> *I personally am very pessimistic about the hope that humanity's disregard for animals will end soon. I'm sometimes afraid that we are approaching an epoch when the hunting of human beings may become a sport. But it is good that there are some people who express a deep protest against the killing and torturing of the helpless, playing with their fears of death, enjoying their misery. Even if God nor nature sides with the killers, the vegetarian is saying: "I protest the ways of God and man." We may admire God's wisdom, but we are not obliged to praise what seems to us His lack of mercy. It may be that somewhere the Almighty has an answer for what He is doing. It may be that one day we shall grasp His answer. But as long as we don't understand it, we shouldn't agree and we shouldn't flatter Him.*
>
> *As long as human beings will go on shedding the blood of animals, there will never be any peace. There is only one little step from killing animals to creating gas chambers a la Hitler and concentration camps a la Stalin—all such deeds are done in the name of "Social Justice." There will*

be no justice as long as man will stand with a knife or with a gun and destroy those who are weaker than he is. (from Forward to Vegetarianism: A Way of Life, by Dudley Geyo) and (*The Extended Circle: A Common Place Book of Animal Rights*)

These powerful words from the hearts of many human beings I have included to empower this subject of vegetarianism. May they be used mightily to touch other hearts. But I have not included why I know and believe that to stop killing and eating all creatures is a deeply spiritual matter. That truth I learned through my own personal experiences, not just through these collected quotations and my extensive reading. And this is why my commitment to vegetarianism is irrevocable. I shall share my experiences now.

CHAPTER THIRTEEN

❖

The Commitment

"The only way to live is to live and let live."
—Mahatma K. Gandhi

"Thou shalt not kill."
—Exodus 20:13

O N September 27, 1989, I became a vegetarian. Perhaps I should begin this testimony and statement by sharing some passages, not all, of the very simple journal entry I made regarding this.

New Hampshire

I am writing in green because it seems to represent nature, and what I am about to enter has to do with nature. "Green is life," and this entry is about life—the life of animals and my life. From this moment on, as I make this entry, I am going to be a vegetarian. I will not eat meat of any kind, nor fish. I cannot let any living creature be killed for my sake, that I might have food. I have not eaten red meat for many years, and for a time I gave up turkey and chicken. But always through family and circumstance and my own weakness, I went back to eating poultry. Though I cannot eat it after I prepare it myself and think it gross—and though I have given up preparing it—I can eat it in restaurants and at others' homes. This is wrong, and I have been going against what I believe. I will also not eat fish, for fish are living creatures too.

I knew the health reasons for giving up all of these things, due to studying the macrobiotic diet, but always I felt, too, that it was wrong to kill animals for our food. Since Rochester has come into my life, the Lord has given me a deepening love for all creatures, sometimes to the point of tears. To think of them being slaughtered in horrendous ways now drives me wild. I always wanted more spiritual evidence that this was wrong, and yet others would say, when it was discussed, that animals were killed in the Bible—and men then ate meat, etc.

I did not have evidence for what I felt personally. This conviction has been growing in me for long time. Suddenly, last Saturday, when at the book sale at the library and I was preparing to leave, I saw a book on the table called Higher Taste*—and it was about the vegetarian way of life. I took it, bought it, and once I began to read, in it I found the answers I have been searching for, and I became convicted in my spirit. I knew I could not now know what I do and continue to eat poultry and fish.*

The scriptural evidence was there that I needed, plus many other facts about cruelty to animals and their suffering, and the way our lives should be lived. I have been reading it each day and cannot go on as I was. I have to become a vegetarian and respect the lives of my fellow creatures.

Please dear Jesus, give me strength to never go backwards, even in the face of criticism or lack of understanding of family or friends. I must do as the Holy Spirit has led me to do. Shortly I will share this with Bob, and I beg you to prepare his heart that he might understand. Thank you, dear Jesus. And I do this too, in deepest gratitude for the gift of Rochester in my life, who has a soul just as I have, and I want to honor him. Help me, dear Jesus. Thank you. Amen.

And I did share this with Bob, and through my prayers that preceded our discussion, he accepted my decision and commitment, and in time—a period of months—he joined me in the vegetarian way. Actually, my commitment had been silently made in my heart on September 26, the previous day, the eleventh anniversary of my mother's death. But we were en route to New Hampshire from Pennsylvania and spent most of the day in the van, and so I did not enter my commitment in writing until the following day, the twenty-seventh, and made it official by my journal entry.

This segment of my spiritual journey actually traces back to 1983, when I read another book, which I can only describe in its affect on me as being almost comparable to having been confronted with Christ, in that I had to make a decision. I could not simply put the book aside when finished and go on as usual with my life. I had been given new knowledge that demanded a response, and I responded in the only way my heart would let me. I said "yes." The book was *Recalled by Life,* by Dr. Anthony Sattilaro, a Catholic physician who was head of Methodist Hospital in Philadelphia. It was his written testimony of being healed of cancer that was all through his body, by adopting and living on the macrobiotic diet. I also identified with him, because his life was changed in the summer of 1978 due to the diagnosis of his illness, the death of his father, and the meeting of strangers who brought him the message of life with the news of this life-giving diet. My life too had been changed that same summer and into the fall just as his had, for I had the miracle given me that I could become a Catholic—a calling I had had in my soul for some years, followed by the death of my mother and then my actual reception into the Catholic Church. That the author also lived in Philadelphia was another tie. Shortly after completing the book, two of my daughters and I, along with many others we knew, were privileged to hear Dr. Sattilaro speak at a local Methodist Church. That night, in a deeply spiritual way, he shared his testimony in even more depth than in the book and showed before-and-after x-rays of his body—the before ones filled with cancer and the after ones revealing the absence of it. Following the talk, he identified, for many people in the audience, illnesses and physical problems that existed in their bodies, through the unusual method of Oriental diagnosis. This is the same method that all macrobiotic counselors use when diagnosing conditions in people who come to them to be put on the macrobiotic diet for healing or prevention of illnesses. Many illnesses that Dr. Sattilaro diagnosed were confirmed right then to him by the people concerned, that they indeed had these conditions. Others were not aware that they had certain problems until he told them; they were then advised to see their own physicians concerning them.

This evening I have long remembered, and I have reread Dr. Sattilaro's book at various times and given it to many others. He went on to write several more books and travelled all over the world to spread hope to others concerning the life-giving macrobiotic diet. Therefore, when I learned the news last year that Dr. Sattilaro had died, I was deeply saddened and felt as if I had lost a friend. I do not know his cause of death, but even if cancer again appeared, he had been given twelve more years of life from his original diagnosis of cancer, and he had used those twelve years to give hope and healing to countless others through his books, travels, and lectures. He left a legacy to all who will listen, and we heard him tell that night in the Methodist Church of how his spiritual life had been deepened, and how he had been a fallen-away Catholic but had returned to the church and even to the attending of daily Mass and the reading of the Breviary.

I have written previously how my macrobiotic cooking lessons helped others, for once I read *Recalled by Life,* I found a macrobiotic center and enrolled in the course. I only wish I had been more strict through the years, for though we still maintain the basics and eat in a vegetarian way, we do not eat a strict macrobiotic diet. But perhaps we shall come full circle and one day embrace it again; in the meantime, there is little of it that we are not using, and always we have short grain brown rice and beans and vegetables. I feel privileged to have had Dr. Sattilaro and the macrobiotic knowledge enter my life, and if I had done it only for my dear little Peruvian friend Magdalena, it would have been worthwhile—for she was given two-and-a-half years of life that she never could have had without it. She had been sent home from the hospital to die. There was nothing any physician could do for her, but the Great Physician opened my eyes to this diet through *Recalled by Life,* and Magdalena's life was recalled for several more years. Praise God! It is our loss that we are not strict in the diet at the present, but that is now. Who is to say what will be? And I pray that readers will truly consider this way and read this powerful book by Dr. Sattilaro, and be open to Our Lord's words to you through his writings. I hope your lives will be touched and changed as my life was. A fine explanation of this diet in a brief way is this one by Bill Tara:

> *The diet which serves us best will be one which produces health and limits disease, is capable of being grown and produced by natural methods, and produces adequate food for all the people of the world.*

It does not involve the killing, torture, and slaughtering of living creatures.

The name *macrobiotics* is derived from the Greek, incidentally; MACRO means great, BIO means vitality, and BIOTICS, the techniques of rejuvenation. I wish to say that in all my years of preparing meals for my large family, it was during the period that I cooked strictly in the macrobiotic way that I enjoyed cooking the most. I also found it most fulfilling, because I knew I was giving the highest form of nourishment to my family. Even though the preparation of each meal took much longer than regular meal preparation of a normal diet, it was the happiest time of my life in regard to cooking. My finest advice to any reader at this point is to learn above all to cook rice and to cook it well— short grain organic brown rice. This is the type that is obtained in a health food store, not in a supermarket. This rice contains all the elements our bodies need, and one can live on it exclusively, as is proven. My husband and I did spend ten days on it alone, and the benefits were incredible. But eating rice regularly would be a beginning for any reader into the vegetarian way. One does not have to be macrobiotic. But brown rice should be in every vegetarian diet, as well as every non-vegetarian diet.

And now, with my personal background written, I would like to relate some unusual happenings that occurred once I made my spiritual commitment to Our Lord—that I would no longer eat, buy, prepare, or cook any living creature again. Never since that day has any creature been served in our home—no matter who is there for dinner. And what followed that commitment only confirmed to me that this truly was a promise made in the spiritual realm, for I was to be tested to the limits of my strength.

Life-Threatening Fear

From that first night, September 27, 1989, I began to have trouble breathing. This was a problem that I have had in my life for some years— not due to allergies but asthma-like difficulties when I am inwardly or emotionally upset. I can go months without problems, only to have them return out of the blue when I am deeply disturbed.

At the time of the commitment, I was totally free of this effect and had been for a long time. But that night, it became evident that the problem was back, and I could not understand why, because I was almost exhilarated over the promise I had made to Our Lord. The first night was not extremely severe, but enough that I took the medication that I use for these times. Several nights that followed were the same, except that breathing was becoming more difficult. Always it began in late evening.

After the first few evenings, the attacks began earlier in the evening. Then I began to experience fear—but I did not know why. Fear of losing my breath, yes, but I would also experience fear while not having these attacks. I would walk into the kitchen area, and suddenly, overwhelming fear would come over me and I would feel cold, and I began to have periods of crying. Soon the attacks began even earlier, and whole evenings were wiped out for me as I struggled to breathe. Even the medication was not helping, and that caused more concern. Finally, my fear deepened so that I was afraid to be left alone in the kitchen or bathroom, which are right outside our bedroom in this small cottage. Once my husband entered the bedroom and left me alone outside of it for any reason, panic rose in me. I would call out to him the best I could, while gasping for breath, and he would hurry to me to take me into the bedroom. But I could not lie down, because I could not breathe if I did. Night after night, I sat on the side of the bed, trying to get my every breath and not even being able to freely let all the tears flow that were in me—for one short of breath cannot afford the luxury of crying. I was so afraid that I could barely swallow or breathe; add to this that we are a mile back into the woods on a lake, with no hospital closer than twenty-five miles. Anyone who has had severe asthma attacks can understand what I am trying to explain. The fear grew deeper, even affecting me during the day, and the attacks began now in the daylight, and the unreasonable fear would rise up in me even when my breathing was free. Finally one Saturday, we drove some distance and bought an inhaler, and that night I had the worst attack I have ever had. It seemed that buying the preventative caused more fear in me than I had ever experienced—this while simply standing in my own kitchen—and followed by a night I am trying to forget, one in which I did not think I would live through until morning. I was so filled with fear that I was afraid to even stop trying for one moment on my own to gasp for breath to let the inhaler be used! I was afraid to put my mouth on it to even have it help me. I felt paralyzed in fear. There was no answer except to pray, as my husband had been doing all along, and as had I for myself. But he put me in the bedroom chair and opened the window over me, wrapping me warmly, and there I sat through the night, literally gasping for every breath. This is the night I recorded briefly in a previous chapter, when I described how my beloved Rochester never left my lap, even to grasping my hands with his little paws. I felt his comfort and presence in a supernatural way. This went on for hours, until something miraculous happened, as a result of our prayers, and I drifted off to sleep until the sunny morning. With Rochester still on my lap, I was breathing normally, and I felt like I had literally been to hell and back.

Many times during that long night I repeated the child's prayer, "Now I Lay Me Down to Sleep." It did not seem to help. My thoughts seemed to center on the words, "If I should die before I wake"—and afforded me no comfort. Later on when discussing this with my husband, we decided to write a replacement prayer that would give us some true comfort and better express what our thoughts were in a nightly conversation with God. Bob surprised me one day with a new prayer, and it was so perfect for me that I did not want to add any other words to it. It is consoling to us both—and I also whisper it every night for Rochester.

> As I lay down to sleep this night,
> Please keep me safe 'til morning light.
> Grant me sleep and needed rest
> And fill my dreams with happiness.
> For Lord, I know that with You near,
> There's nothing that I have to fear.
> Please guide me where You want to lead,
> And be with those I love and need.

And it was that morning when the Holy Spirit impressed upon my soul, as I sat there utterly bedraggled and exhausted from hours of fighting to breathe, that I was being attacked by the evil one—the devil—and that these days and nights of uncontrollable fear and gasping for breath had been filled with spiritual warfare! I was in awe, and it was incredulous to me when it was first revealed to me, but the fact is I accepted it immediately as utter truth, confirming to me that, indeed, the Holy Spirit had spoken within my being. Insights came flooding in on me at the time of this revelation, regarding things that had occurred in the past week and a half. Every time I had made a journal entry, from the very first one concerning my commitment, I had been attacked. The attacks began subtly at first, but then began to occur almost immediately after each entry. Then, every time I wrote a letter to a friend about my decision, I felt the repercussions of my sharing, following it. Attack after attack! If I spoke to anyone on the phone regarding what I had done—again I was struck. Fear is not of God, and I realized all the unreasonable fear and cold that came over me were from the evil one. The buying of the inhaler to help myself brought on the severest attack of all, even to paralyzing me so I could not use it even once! Suddenly, when at my weakest, in the early morning following the worst night I remembered— the Holy Spirit spoke to me. Perhaps He had before, but I had not heard. When we are weak, then He is strong, and I felt His strength and wisdom and presence in the revelations He revealed. It was frightening, yet now I knew and could fight back.

This was not my first experience with the evil one in a very real way; instances immediately came back to me. I had brought along to New Hampshire from Pennsylvania on this last trip a new Crucifix, meant to be hung on the wall. It was at least twelve inches long and seven inches wide, with heavy wood trimmed around the edges with ornate silver. It was very beautiful, and I intended it to be hung over our bed, but we had not yet done that. I took that Crucifix and carried it with me everywhere about the house. No matter where I was or what I was doing, I carried the Crucifix. First my husband and I had prayed, strongly denouncing the evil one, and in the name of Jesus Christ we cast him and his demons into the void. And then I had blessed myself with Holy Water, which I had been doing frequently even before, and blessed each room with the Holy Water—and the Crucifix became my constant companion. Eventually my husband tried to lighten me up a bit after all I had been through, and he placed the large Crucifix on a red cord and hung it about my neck. He told me I looked as fine as the Pope. And, ridiculous though it may sound to some readers who have never experienced such attacks, I wore this with my Hemingway sweatshirt as I sat at my desk writing, and I wore it when I cooked, read—no matter what—and I wore it to bed. It was then I felt the need of it most. With Rosary in hand, Crucifix lying the length of my body on a red cord, and Rochester lying on my legs—I was a sight to behold. But I felt no more fear, from that first morning when the Holy Spirit had revealed the truth to me—and there were no more breathing problems during the weeks that followed. I was able to write about the commitment and witness to it in my journal or letters, and my breathing remained normal. Every day we prayed, and I took nothing for granted. We kept a close spiritual watch and vigil on the entire thing. Toward the end of our stay, when we had to return to Pennsylvania for a brief period of a couple weeks, we first hung the Crucifix over our bed, where it had been intended to be, and during the drive back to Pennsylvania I held a small wooden crucifix in my hand. The next day I went to our Catholic Shop and bought quite a large Crucifix to wear around my neck always, in addition to a medal of the Blessed Mother's, which I never removed. From that day on I have worn the Crucifix as protection. It was a battle I will never forget, and I know the evil one was truly out to harm me because of the promise I had made and because I was regularly witnessing to it. We knew without a doubt that we had been engaged in severe spiritual warfare with the evil one. And it was very obvious to us that this happened because I no longer could allow myself to eat living creatures or even have one killed so that I might live. And the evil one—who loves the evil of slaughtering and torture and all the horrors connected with the horrendous deaths of millions of creatures—was fighting me at every turn and striking me at my weakest point, my breathing! Putting unreasonable fear into me was the beginning of the many attacks, then using my point of vulnerability to frighten me even more, so that I would give in and go back to being a cause of living beings being slaughtered for my food. But he had lost the battle, because I fought in the power of Jesus Christ, and I won. I will always remember my wonderful friend Monsignor Flatley's words, telling me one night long before these attacks, that *"in the face of evil, hold up a Crucifix, and the devil will depart."* The Holy Spirit had brought those words to my remembrance, and I had obeyed, and I had won! Soon after, I was impressed to write this book, and I knew I could never write it unless I included this testimony, so that any who follow after me and make the decision to, as Thoreau stated, "leave off eating meat" will be forewarned that a spiritual battle may ensue if you are not prepared as I have described. If it is a spiritual commitment to you, and you are doing it as a moral act for God and for all living creatures—and not merely for a healthy diet—then you must be prepared, pray much, and protect yourself from evil. In addition to my husband who went through it all with me, I shared this in every detail with a Holy Christian friend, Dan, and he proclaimed without a doubt that the evil one was fighting me all the way through my spiritual walk and commitment, and indeed I had been waging and was caught up in spiritual warfare. Never doubt! It is real! Stay close to Our Lord and be protected. The evil one never wants good or life—only evil and death.

Yes, I have had other times since when I could not breathe properly, but these occurred when my emotions were abused and I had been betrayed by someone I had trusted but who was truly caught up in evil. And again I waged spiritual warfare. But these times I recognized at once what was happening, and the result was different. I will always know when this happens, from now on, because of those weeks in the fall of 1989 and what the Holy Spirit revealed to me.

For months I put off writing this chapter and testimony. First, I would not write it while it snowed here in the woods, and then there were other reasons. I even joked that perhaps I should write it while sitting in a hospital lobby, in case the evil one struck out. Even this night as I have been writing I have been apprehensive, as it has come to final countdown when I had to at last get it all down on paper for my book. But the testimony is completed now, and I am covered by prayer, and my Rosary is here on my desk, my Crucifix around my neck, and my large Crucifix hanging above the bed where I will sleep tonight. And I know that Our Lord is pleased that I have at long last set this down so that other readers might know and realize that it is no slight thing to murder, torture, slaughter, hunt, and experiment on helpless animals. It is no slight matter when even one life is taken—human or creature. This experience has been engraved on my soul, and I know with all my being that it is immoral to murder another whose life you yourself can never replace. Therefore, my lifestyle and diet can never be responsible for another's death. My commitment is irrevocable, as is my husband's, and I know it to be truth: *"Thou shalt not kill"*—not humans, not animals, not any living thing. May the Holy Spirit speak to your souls. The following poem was written October 15, 1989, following my commitment.

Do Unto Others

God in His Creation
Put upon this earth—
A host of marvelous animals
His Breath gave them their worth.

He did not want them slaughtered
He said "Thou shalt not kill"—
He wanted them to live in peace
Not at mercy of men's will.

He gave them woods and pastures
To live in nature's plan—
He did not want them tortured
By insensitivities of man.

He made them fellow creatures
In this universe so great
They were not to fill men's bellies
And be sprawled across a plate!

Why must they kill such animals
As cow and lamb and pig—
Innocents cannot fight back
Oh men—you're not so big!

And what of jungle animals?
It is becoming clear—
Through senseless killings for great sport
Extinction comes—they disappear!

Do not justify these killings
Oh, you of human race—
Live and let live from this moment
Declare the end to this disgrace!

Close down the slaughterhouses
Let the woods be hunter free—
Repent to God for all these lives—
And then a new world we will see.

In a somewhat lighter vein, I add the following poem, written after Bob answered an ad in a local New Hampshire newspaper and planned to give me a gift of a lovely green leather sofa. It was like new and a color we both admired. But I could not accept it, and as a result I wrote this in fun for Bob. How could I sit comfortably on such a sofa, enjoying myself, while writing a book of this sort and having just made a spiritual commitment? Besides, the lumpy old sofa held dear memories for me, as I have mentioned in a previous chapter.

No, Thank You

It was a sofa that he tried
To give me—made of animal hide.
Made from a creature meant to roam—
And not to be inside our home.

It fit our needs so perfectly
And yet I had to disagree—
It could not come and fill the space—
Of older piece—now a disgrace.

A luxury, yes—and lovely green
But how compassionless, and mean
To add to slaughter of this cow
Deny commitments—weakly bow—

Just to have a sofa new
And own green leather soft—could you?
And he agreed with this—and now
Our sofa's still of lumps—not cow!

And this next poem was written on the second anniversary of my
commitment, affirming anew that my decision is irrevocable.

The Commitment

Two years ago I did commit—
Stopped being then a hypocrite.
No longer could I say I care—
While eating creatures for my fare.
If animals I loved so dearly—
Then I had to say quite clearly,
That vegetarianism I'd embrace—
And not eat anything with a face.

Red meat I gave up long ago—
Dear lambs and cows I did forego.

All creatures in that category—
Became absolutely mandatory—
To exclude—I could not bear,
Their slaughter and the deep nightmare—
That they endured so I might eat—
When eating meat is obsolete!

Suddenly I knew I could not—
Eat fish or poultry—no, I would not!
For they are creatures God gave life—
Not meant for strife and human knife—
But to survive; remain alive.
Can I as human thrive, deprive,
A being of its right to live—
When there is known alternative?

I eat now beans and much brown rice;
Good fresh vegetables—perhaps a slice—
Of bread—and yes, spaghetti's nice—
It really is not sacrifice—
And yet each day I have a feast—
But not on fish or fowl or beast.
But now my soul does not protest.
For on my plate there is no guest!

Rochester
in summer, enjoying
his (our) porch

CHAPTER FOURTEEN

❖

A Call to Prayer for God's Creatures

"More things are wrought by prayer than this world dreams of.
Wherefore, let thy voice rise like a fountain for me night and day."
—Alfred Lord Tennyson

BECAUSE CHRISTIANS ARE KNOWN as people of prayer, I believe those who truly love and care about animals carry their prayers into the lives of God's creatures, praying for them in general as well as for their specific needs. The accounts that follow are positive happenings that I have been involved in personally or have read about.

Approximately nineteen years ago, on a number of occasions, several of us prayed for a lovely golden retriever who was ill. I do not remember the nature of the illness each time now, but the dog was a beloved companion to our minister friend and his wife. We would ask Goldie to lie on the floor on her side, and those of us involved would kneel around her and "lay hands" on her, just as we would for a human. She felt our love and the warmth from our hands as the Holy Spirit moved through us and touched and healed her. This should not be an uncommon or unusual occurrence. It should be completely normal. We should pray for and with our animal friends and companions, just as we would for our human family and friends.

A dear friend, Dan, whom I mentioned previously, who had a beloved German Shepherd companion named Heidi, prayed for my

Rochester during a brief period when I thought he was ill, due to a veterinarian who mistakenly led me to believe that there was a great chance that Rochester was indeed ill. In addition to praying for Rochester, my friend authored a beautiful, tender, spiritual writing, to ease my emotional pain and apprehensions as I awaited the results from a test that had been done on Rochester. I found the paper tucked under my front door knocker, with no name signed, the afternoon of the day that I had asked him to pray. It gave me hope and strength, and I grew stronger with each rereading of it and through his prayers. My family and several other close friends were praying also. I knew the writing was from this man the minute I saw the paper under the knocker, and upon reading it, this was confirmed in my spirit. This was such an act of love. No fanfare, no signature—just a giving of self in a quiet way. Though I have included it in a previous book, *Higher Ground*, I would like again to include it here, for I pray there are many new readers that can gain comfort from this sensitive and loving missal. My friend called it a "Musing," and I have been blessed from time to time since this original musing to receive additional "musings" from him on various Christian subjects. They arrive in the mail as sweet surprises to bring me encouragement. A later chapter of this book contains another musing by him.

Now may you be blessed as I was through Dan's gift of writing and prayer.

Musings on the Sacred Heart of Jesus and Pussy Cats

Jesus Christ, son of man, was all man as well as all God.

When Jesus ascended to be with the Father, he ascended with the heart of man, a human heart. Thus a human heart became part of the Godhead, a heart like ours, one that has lived and loved and experienced joy, pain, and grief, just as have we.

You may be assured that Jesus loved pussy cats—and all the other pets and animal companions God gave to us to delight our heart and give us companionship and comfort.

It is not silly to pray for a pussy cat. It is an act of trust and faith to ask our Father to cure our sick pet and enable us to continue to delight in our love of His gift of the pussy cat. Remember, if His eye is on the sparrow, you know it is also on your pussy cat.

Therefore:

Father in heaven, through the Human Heart of Jesus, hear my prayer and make my pussy cat well, for you know full well the anguish I experience when I consider that he may be taken from me. In Jesus' name, Amen.

—Daniel T. Deane, Jr.

Prayer Rituals for Healing

I have just spoken of the incident concerning Rochester and what occurred as we awaited the result of his blood test, but I did not specifically share the details of my personal prayers on his behalf. Dan, who wrote the musing, was indeed praying, as were Bob, family members, and several friends who also loved animals. But privately I was soaking Rochester in prayer more than ever and claiming the verse of Hebrews 11:1 as my support scripture ally:

What is faith? It is the confident assurance that something we want is going to happen. It is the certainty of what we hope for is waiting for us, even though we cannot see it up ahead.

For outward evidence of this and something tangible I could see and touch, I made myself a drawing of the Sacred Heart of Jesus, a large heart with a flame above it. Inside the heart I drew a glass vial containing Rochester's blood sample. On the paper I wrote, *"Thank you, Jesus, for the gift of Rochester's perfect blood test,"* and I wrote out the entire scripture verse. I also wrote, *"O Sacred Heart of Jesus, I place my Trust in Thee."* I placed this picture on what I call my altar table in my prayer room, which holds significant statues and pictures of Our Lord, Our Lady of Lourdes, and several Saints. Repeatedly I knelt there at the table, placing my hand on the paper, thanking Jesus in advance for the perfect test result, and always ending with *"O Sacred Heat of Jesus, I place my trust in Thee."* I cannot describe the peace that came to my soul as I continued to do this over and over many times each day and evening while I waited out the four days until the veterinarian was to call.

I also made other papers like it, with the same drawing of the Sacred Heart and the same prayers and scripture, and gave them to my husband, who kept his before him on his desk as he worked, and to other family members, the author of the musing, and to my friends who were specifically praying. It was a note about Rochester that contained this drawing to my friend Dan (who gave me such incredible comfort through his caring and musing)—that led him to write the musing in response. I grew in strength in those four days, and I "laid hands" on Rochester many times in prayer. No matter when he was on my lap, which was frequently, I prayed for him also, asking the Holy Spirit to send His Healing Power through him and to make his blood perfect and every part of his little body within and without perfect.

By the time the call came that Monday night—having waited since Thursday morning—I could lift the receiver in confidence and I believed without a doubt that I would hear that his blood test was perfect. And it was! This prayer also restored Chester in another way—for when he had been taken for his check-up Thursday morning, we had left him for the operation to have him neutered. I had been so anxious over this also—and had delayed longer than usual to have this necessary surgery done. When we received him back into our arms later Thursday afternoon—though utterly distressed over the news of this possible blood problem—I saturated him in prayer also for his healing from his neutering. He was so tired and unlike himself, and it frightened me. But the continual prayer and love through my "laying on of hands" and other prayers brought him back to being his active playful self in a very short time. It is a four- to five-day period I will never forget.

But Rochester is not only prayed for in times when I think something is amiss! He is prayed for every day of his life and is surrounded by an aura of prayer that I am always sending up. And many times a day as I hold him, I pray for him and ask that love and healing and strength be sent to every cell of his small body by the power of the Holy Spirit. All our personal animal companions should receive daily loving prayer, not only for them but directly upon them with "laying on of hands" by their loved ones. It should be as normal as if praying for our beloved human family and friends. I also pray for Rochester daily through the Rosary, usually at night as he cuddles down with me. This is a form of prayer I felt led to do in gratitude to Our Lord and Blessed Mother for his complete recovery.

Each night I also make the Sign of the Cross on his little forehead and give him this blessing before he sleeps. It is a blessing I have given each of my six children for years at bedtime and that I began at once to give him when he was adopted and became mine. I also make this Sign on him if I have to be away from him for a few hours, always accompanied by a little kiss in the same spot, of course.

In those times when I have to be gone a few hours longer and Bob and I are away together while Rochester is alone, I always have moments when I am quiet and visualize him at peace and secure in the knowledge that we will be back soon. I send him little love messages in prayer and believe that he is receiving them as I envision him at home. I also leave clothing articles of Bob's and mine on the bed where he sleeps, so that he can feel our presence too, through being with these or snuggling down into them. He is particularly fond of my bath robe, and that truly is a comfort to him.

Almost three years ago, not long after the situation with Rochester when I called upon the Sacred Heart, I was asked by my friends Peggy and Gina to come to their home to pray with their sick cat who had a problem with kidney stones. I went to my friends' home, and there together Peggy and I ministered to this sweet little companion. Gina could not be present. Little Felicity sat on my lap while I "laid hands" on her and prayed for some time and left a drawing of the Sacred Heart as I had made for my own little Rochester—so that the drawing would aid · in their prayers each day for Felicity. I also left a tape of "The Fairy Ring," unusual music that has significant meaning to me, so that my friends might use it in meditation and when holding their little cat. While there, we had prayer for their dog Dawn Alice also. To those who love their companions, this should not seem an unusual occurrence—to minister to these little ones who are in pain or who are ill. My friends who loved and cared for Felicity and Dawn Alice, and their other cat Luanne, devotedly prayed with their little Felicity thereafter, just as they had always done before I visited. But as Scripture says, *"Where two or three are gathered together in my name, there am I in their midst."* From that time on, my friends tried these other forms of prayer that I had shared that day, with Peggy, as well as their own ways. Their little cat did not live for very long, for the veterinarian decided she had to be put to sleep, even though she was only a young cat. It broke our hearts, but we had the comfort of knowing that to the very end my friends gave their companion both prayer and spiritual attention. And this dear little Felicity truly knew, despite her pain, that she was indeed loved very much.

In the past I prayed in a regular way with our three little Cairn Terriers, and in times of illness, especially when the little lady dogs, Lizzie and Muffin, had to have tumors removed. I know my daughter Jessica prayed with her Katie, too, as did I.

Animals are so much like humans when they become ill—at least certainly those who live in homes with their humans. My little Rochester is comforted by my holding him and by my prayers and stroking when he becomes car sick on the very first and last miles of his frequent trips to New Hampshire. He travels over 400 miles and in the first few minutes as we settle in the van he throws up in anxiety, and in the last mile he throws up due to the winding country road that approaches our woods and cottage. I carry a little plastic dish, which he neatly uses to throw up in while standing in his carrier that is strapped to my seat belt and that sits on my lap. Then he lies down and I put my arm in and hold him in his carrier and lovingly pet him. He holds onto my arm with outstretched paw. It is very tender. I comfort him in this way throughout the long trip. I recently wrote a poem describing what takes place when we make these very frequent trips, for we spend most of our time in New Hampshire, but travel back and forth continuously.

TRAVELING AMBASSADOR

When we get in the van to travel—
Rochester starts then to unravel.
Under his chin I place a cup—
Into which he must throw up.
Once that's over he lies down—
And we're ready to leave town.

He is secure within his carrier—
Strapped to my seat belt—it's a barrier,
Against the dangers as we drive—
He is quite safe 'til we arrive.

Four hundred miles and more we go—
No impatience does he show.
Now we drive across the line—
Into New Hampshire—State so fine.
As we cruise up One-fifty-three—
So filled with hills and turns—then he—
Needs again that little cup
Into which he must throw up.
And then we make just one more swerve—
Heading 'round our final curve.

And while Rochester's tummy sinks—
He knows these roads are final links—
To the woods and lake and trees—
Now his little heart's at ease—
For soon he'll be where he loves most,
The little cottage where he's host—
To birds and wildlife who will stare
Through screens and windows for they care,
That Rochester has returned once more.
The little goodwill ambassador!

Dedicated to
Rochester Harry Whittier Kolb,
Famous Feline Traveler

When Animals Need Mothering Love

My daughter Jessica's Katie was such a little child. One of the sweetest memories we have of her caused us to laugh often. A number of times, at least four or five, Katie had an upset stomach while my daughter was either at school or work. Why it should have always happened while I was in my Prayer Room, I do not know, but it did. Katie would run upstairs to me (if not already with me) when sick, and each time before I could remove things from my lap and jump up to lead her into the bathroom, she would look in my face with pitiful eyes, and I knew what was coming. She would throw up at my feet, all over my new blue shag rug and my shoes. I can still hear myself excitedly saying, "*No no, Katie! Wait a minute!—Wait a minute!*" But she never could. She came to tell me she was sick and then proved it! Even though my rug took a beating, it was funny. She needed her "Grandmom," since her Mom was not around. I would always worry then that she was really ill, but once she threw up she was better. Then I would put my hands on her head and pray. I would talk to her, and as I would clean up the mess and she would watch, we would have "heart-to-hearts" about *where* she would throw up next time she became nauseated. She was a little girl and she needed me. She did not run off to a place alone and do it.

Animals need our love and prayers and sympathy when ill. We are their loved ones—their people.

"The Fairy Ring"

Eight summers ago, while vacationing at Acadia National Park, my friend was standing outdoors at a point where she was in view of Cadillac Mountain. In awe she beheld the sight, which captivated her and drew her into deep contemplation. While in this state, she began to hear music, music so beautiful that it seemed not to be of this world. She continued to listen while gazing at this magnificent view and said that these were moments she will always remember. At last she felt she must learn the source of the lovely strains. She searched it down until she discovered a gift shop not far from where she had been standing. A cassette tape being played was sending this unusual music out into the open to join with nature. Ruth asked about the music and then purchased two tapes. She brought them home, and several different mornings after Mass when we were having coffee and prayer together, she told me that I must hear one of the tapes and that she would bring one to me. At last she did, and I have been ever grateful for this gift. Thus began a portion in my life that has been so precious—for this music has calmed my soul nightly for almost eight years. From the first time I took Ruth's tape off to a room alone to listen, I was overwhelmed by the beauty of the music. It was not like any other music I had ever heard before. It was flowing and continuous, for almost a half hour, and the reverse side held even more beauty. It was like heavenly music, super-naturally beautiful, and I just wanted to listen to it over and over. It was called "The Fairy Ring." Even the name was unusual.

I do not exaggerate when I say that from that day on, I have played this tape every single night once I am in bed. Usually I listen in the dark, but occasionally before I turn out the light I also play it as I write in my journal and then continue to play it in the dark. I never listen to it at any other time, for to me it is not background music to work by nor music listened to while talking or driving. It is played only at night and the only others who share that music with me in my presence are Bob and Rochester. They are often awake when it begins but asleep before it finishes. No one talks through it. It is music for the night and aloneness—and I do not understand its hold on me. I know only that the haunting, mystical strains nurture my soul and are like healing balm—only the Lord knows just why this music ministers to me so. I share all this in depth, because I want you to realize that our animal companions are so much like we are, and they too, can be ministered to in ways that we are.

An example of this, one that revealed new insights to me as to how I might soothe and help my own little companion as well as other animals, was shown me one night in Pennsylvania. We had just arrived there after our long trip down from New Hampshire, after being up north for many weeks. We felt rather lost at leaving the lake, the woods, the solitude, and the work we had been doing every day, to return to the busyness and different lifestyle waiting for us in Pennsylvania. This is always a difficult transition for me, no matter how often I return to Pennsylvania. Going in the opposite direction brings a wonderful opposite feeling to my soul, and the feeling is all joy when we head back up north.

This particular night, as we returned to Pennsylvania, was the same as all others, except we had been away for a longer period than usual. Once there, I let little Chester out of his carrier to roam and to have his dinner and fresh water. After Bob and I looked at the mail, it was time for bed. Bob fell asleep immediately, but I stayed awake to read and write. Chester did not climb up on the bed with me but continued to roam. This was totally out of character, even after a long, confining trip. I lifted him onto the bed with me, but he immediately jumped down. This continued several more times. I finally turned out the light, believing he would come and lie down as always. But he did not. He went from window to window, looking out into the night, and I heard him repeating this frequently. Then he wandered into the adjoining bathroom, and I heard him on the sill, rustling the curtain. Then he was in the tub. All about the two rooms he wandered, totally restless and unsettled. Because I know him so deeply, this was really not normal, and of course, then I began to worry that he did not feel well. All manner of negative thoughts crossed my mind as I sat in the dark, disturbed that he was not there with me as always, asleep on my legs in bed. I began to pray for him, and as I did I was suddenly given the needed insight in such a forceful way that I was amazed! It was revealed to me by the Holy Spirit that Chester was unsettled because he had been away from this home and surroundings for so long—and that I had forgotten something very important that would make him feel at peace at once: I had forgotten to put on the cassette tape of "The Fairy Ring" for the very first time since I had owned it! And the reason I had not put it on, I am sure, was because my little one's behavior was not as it always was, and I was so concerned and so awake that it had not come to that point in my schedule to turn on the music. I did so immediately and just sat quietly. Within a few seconds I heard Chester jump down from a window sill, cross the room, and hop up on the bed. He walked the length of me to bump his little head into mine a number of times, then circled around and curled up on me. Never did he move again! Everything was as it always is every night. And when I awoke to go to Mass, he was still asleep, and I had to slide out so as not to disturb him.

I had forgotten to put on the music that ministered to his soul also, which had become such an integrated part of our bedtime ritual that he was totally lost without it and restless in the surroundings he had not been in for so long. This was a beautiful lesson to be shown—that our souls respond in the same way to this haunting, supernatural music, and that we both felt out of sorts when we had to leave New Hampshire. Perhaps this story will help other readers in ministering to their animal companions.

Should any reader find the true stories I have related here to be unusual or that prayer seems not right for animals, let me assure you that prayer is as correct for animals as it is for us. God created us all, and therefore we should always include our dear animal companions in our prayers, and also pray for all the animals in the world that they be spared cruelty. Pray for all their needs as the Holy Spirit leads you.

A Book of Prayers for Animals

I own two copies of a very loving book, *Bless All Thy Creatures, Lord*, so that I might never be without it. I keep one copy in New Hampshire and one in Pennsylvania and have given it to many friends who also love and care about animals. It is a book of "Prayers for Animals," compiled by Richard Newman, a Presbyterian minister who has taught religion and also written a number of books. He has long been active in Animal Welfare. The prayers in the book are from all traditions, collected by him and also sent to him by others. He credits many others known personally to him—a beloved uncle, a woman with a radical approach to Animal Welfare, and another woman at the Catholic Study Center for Animal Welfare in London, an organization that combines a religious perspective with effective activism, as does the Society of United Prayer for Animals. Newman also credits Peter Singer (Animal Liberation) for showing him the philosophical basis for Animal Rights.

And after mention of those who helped him believe in the book, he pays highest tribute to his closest companion of the past eleven years, a female Golden Retriever dog named Phyllis, who lay next to his chair as he wrote the acknowledgments. He states (and freely acknowledges) so tenderly that his greatest debt is to Phyllis, since it was she who taught him the quality of relationships that can exist between animals and people. He also wrote that she would not survive until the book's publication, for she had a wasting arthritic disease that has no cure. This breaks my heart each time I read it. Perhaps this tribute by a Minister of God, paid to his beloved companion, will punctuate all that I have written in truth concerning my relationship with Rochester and other relationships between animals and persons that I have included. I believe you would be blessed by this beautiful book by Richard Newman, and the publisher is Macmillan Publishing Co., Inc. This book is a continual blessing to me and is always on the table next to me. I will quote just one small paragraph from the inside flap of the attractive book cover, which pictures a large tree filled with every sort of God's Creatures:

> Bless All Thy Creatures, Lord *is a book for anyone who has ever enjoyed a leisurely stroll with a dog or played hide-and-seek with a cat. It is for anyone who has felt joy at hearing the bird songs that mark the arrival of dawn, who has been thrilled by the sudden sight of a deer or a rabbit or a fox or who has drawn comfort in time of sadness from the companionship of a beloved pet. It is a book for you—and for every animal lover you know.*

May this very spiritual book come into your life very soon.

A Cat's Healing Brings Renewal of Faith

A beautiful article appeared in the *Catholic Standard and Times Newspaper* several years ago about a sick cat who brought a woman back to her faith and the Catholic Church. It was entitled "A Cat Lives and A Woman Believes" and appeared in the December 4, 1986 issue. It stated that a simple blessing over a dying cat had been credited with saving the pet and restoring the faith of the owner.

This woman's pet had been diagnosed with jaundice, liver failure, and feline leukemia. The cat grew feeble and a yellow tinge began showing through the black fur. The doctor gave the twelve-year-old cat, Sam, a 50/50 chance and a second veterinarian was even less optimistic. Sam could no longer stand. After trying everything she could to help him and save him, she took Sam to the veterinarian on October 2 for a blood test. She was in tears and that night prayed he would die in his sleep, for she could not bear for him to suffer, yet she could not make the decision to have him put to sleep.

On the Feast of St. Francis of Assisi, October 4, she remembered the traditional blessing of animals that some parishes have, and she took Sam in his little carrier to the church where about thirty people had gathered. It was unusual that she should decide to participate in this blessing, because she had had a falling out with a parish priest many years before and had never gone back to church. The blessing ceremony took about fifteen minutes. She took the carrier with Sam in it to a priest, and he blessed the animal with Holy Water. This immediately made a difference to both the little cat and its owner.

The woman felt very peaceful and felt that Sam was safe. In the following days, right before her eyes, she watched her cat grow healthier and stronger, and he began eating again and the jaundice began to fade. On October 19, Sam climbed onto her bed and waited for her to pat him. The woman was overjoyed and could not believe it. Her first impression was that she should go to church, and she did return, for the first time in years, and she heard a sermon on perseverance that spoke directly to her. At that Mass she decided to renew her faith and return to church, and she said it is a promise she intends to keep.

I believe this is evidence of how Our Lord uses our precious animals and through them speaks to us and leads us. I have always saved that article and remembered its story, for it happened the same year that Rochester came into my life, not quite four months later.

The Feast of St. Francis of Assisi

Other churches also have wonderful services of Blessing and Prayer for the animals on the Feast of St. Francis of Assisi every October 4. The massive Cathedral of St. John the Divine in New York is one of these, and a newspaper account several years ago stated that 4,000 worshippers had watched the blessing of a turtle, a camel, an elephant, a snake, a tree, and ocean-going algae, representing species that have suffered man-inspired cruelty.

For the Feast of St. Francis of Assisi, celebrated this year on October 6, the Cathedral of St. John the Divine again had a celebration, but this time it was more colorful, and a joyful celebration of life in all its splendid diversity. So stated the article in the *Boston Globe* by writer Dianne Durmanoski. Clouds of incense curled upward in the Gothic nave as the long soaring howl of a wolf swelled gloriously into the great space. This howl marked the beginning of the Kyrie Eleison in the Earth Mass celebrated annually on this day.

Other voices joined in—a musician on his oboe, a human choir of 300 voices, and a number of inspired dogs in the congregation. St. Francis, the 12th century Italian saint who befriended the wolf of Gubbio and preached about human kinship to other creatures, would certainly be pleased by this exuberant chorus and with the religious community's growing environmental awareness. In the spirit of the good Saint, fellow creatures were again welcome, so the congregation included hundreds of dogs, cats, and birds, as well as a variety of other pets. The Cathedral throbbed with life during the three-hour mass, and the ceremony conveyed the power of ritual, the resonance of ancient symbols, and the transporting beauty of song and dance. Whale songs and African drumming mixed with the medieval pomp of the high Episcopal Church.

The article states that at the climax, the congregation fell silent, and the Cathedral, in an act both literal and symbolic, threw its huge brass doors open to the rest of creation. Down the great central aisle they all came in procession: an elephant with a garland about its neck, a mouse carried by a child, an elegant barn owl, a furry spider, a camel, a cedar tree, rain forest orchids, a hive of bees, and a 3.5-billion-year-old rock from Australia bearing the fossil imprint of blue-green algae, one of the most ancient forms of life.

The article closes by saying that there was a feeling of homecoming—and delight and wonder and mystery.

A man involved with the Vivisection Society said that he came away from the service at St. John the Divine impressed with the power of the church. "Without it, this movement will go nowhere," he stated, "for we are only a brush fire in this cause for animals, and we want to become a conflagration."

Other Church-Based Efforts on Behalf of Animals

Another church in Pennsylvania has an annual service as a reminder that man's dominion over God's non-human creatures implies a benevolent stewardship. This service concludes World Week of Prayer for the Animals, and the pastor of this church states that the Week of Prayer set aside for animals is a week to educate ourselves further as to how we treat animals and to consider a renewed lifestyle—for God, in His Wisdom, created animals for His own pleasure, not for ours.

This Pennsylvania pastor feels that as this movement gains momentum, comparisons will be seen to the abolitionist, civil rights, and women's suffrage struggles, and he believes that virtually every institution involved with animals will be affected. Farmers will stop genetically altering cattle and fowl to increase production; medical researchers and biological testers will cease animal experimentation, and cosmetics firms will look for other ways to test skin products. This kind man of God believes that eventually we may all adopt the ultimate diet for those dedicated to living a compassionate lifestyle. He points out that the Bible says we are to be vegetarians, and he feels it is inconsistent to love a cat or dog and eat a sheep or cow.

He advocates the vegan way of life, which avoids and shuns the consumption of meat, meat by-products, eggs, milk, cheese, or honey. Vegans are those who by decision deal only with "cruelty-free" markets that sell no products resulting from animal suffering. They do not wear animal fur or leather, and this pastor wears all man-made (fiber) shoes.

The international organization, Mobilization for Animals, estimates that 70 million cats, dogs, cows, rabbits, monkeys, and mice are being used unnecessarily for scientific experiments. This pastor's organization, which is affiliated with the American Anti-Vivisection Society and People for the Ethical Treatment of Animals, hopes to put an end to such practices. The pastor has stated that they do not aim merely for a humane attitude toward animals, but they want people to move from admiration for animals to advocacy. This network sees the church as a natural ally. And so, in addition to all this work throughout the year on the behalf of animals, each October the doors of his church swing open on a Sunday afternoon so that an unusual procession may march in. Just as their ancestors filed into the protection and shelter of Noah's Ark, so will dogs, fish, cats, cows, iguanas, donkeys, horses, and others pass with their human protectors into this gray stone church. The pastor states that whatever is brought along will be permitted in and blessed, and that we are all fellow travelers. This pastor is executive director of the International Network for Religion and Animals, a several-thousand-member educational organization whose goal is to show the theological framework for mankind's relationship with animals. I pray for this man and all of his work, that animals may be protected and saved. He has added that all animals have intrinsic value, species have intrinsic value, and that life is precious—and we need to honor that life. He is a Christian who is truly doing God's work in incredible ways.

This past October, during the writing of this book, the Immaculate Conception BVM Church of Jenkintown, Pennsylvania (my own church) for the first time began to bless the animals. On the Feast of St. Francis of Assisi, parishioners with their beloved animal companions assembled in the school yard, and under the loving direction of Father John J. Conahan and Father James F. Endres, Father Endres blessed each animal present. I was in New Hampshire working on this manuscript, and so was not able to attend, but friends from Immaculate Church told me what a wonderful event it was and the warm feeling that was shared between priest and parishioners as the animals were ministered to that afternoon. I was very thankful for this beautiful service, initiated on that Feast Day.

In closing this chapter containing the many influences and personal accounts of prayer for animals, I would like to relate one last story that happened just two weeks ago. To me, this is a true example of prayer between person and animal, but in this situation, the animal was praying for the person. He was praying in the deepest sense of the word, in the only way he knew how, by his utter devotion, continual presence, and a perseverance until the trouble lifted. I can speak with a definite inner knowing, because I experienced this type of prayer as given to me by my beloved Rochester. I referred earlier to a time when he ministered to me through a very frightening night of illness, but this more recent incident was for a much more extended period. However, I am in no way minimizing the devotion and care I received from Chester during *that* earlier crisis. Never!

This time, I was ill for three-and-a-half days, confined to the bedroom. I rarely am sick, but this time I was very sick with some unknown virus plus some emotional upset. I could only stay in bed (as I was nauseated) or sit in a recliner. I was too weak to walk. For three-and-a-half days my little Chester remained with me. Either he was on my legs as I lay in bed, or he was circled on my lap as I sat in the chair. He never left me except for infrequent trips to his litter box and for a little food—both situated in the bathroom adjoining our bedroom. He remained on me and with me all through each night and each day. There is no doubt in my mind that this was a prayer form ministered to me by one who loves me deeply. I cannot begin to tell you what a comfort it was to have this warm little body with me to hold, and to see the love in his eyes and feel his purring. He "kept watch" the entire period until we left to make the trip to New Hampshire when I felt somewhat better. Even though he remained in his carrier on my lap all during the trip north, once he arrived, with his freedom to play and roam, he was instantly back on my lap again. He truly was a ministering angel those three-and-a-half days of sickness, and once in New Hampshire I wrote this poem in tribute to him—for his deep love and caring. I know my Rochester prayed for me!

Guardian Angel

Little being filled with love—
You fit my heart just like a glove—
Revealing soul—in silent gaze—
And constant presence through the days.

Waiting in anticipation—
On bathrobed lap—your chosen station,
You remain—to underscore—
You long that I'll be strong once more.

Golden eyes in concentration
Search my eyes in adoration—
Little paws clasp firm my hand,
Telling me you understand.

Purring me to sleep and rest—
To make me well is your sweet quest.
Guardian Angel in soft fur—
White and marmalade comforter.

Dedicated to
Rochester Harry Whittier Kolb (Chester)

CHAPTER FIFTEEN

❧

Grieving for Our Animal Companions

"Gone from our sight, but never our memories.
Gone from our touch, but never our hearts."
—unknown

THIS IS A VERY DIFFICULT CHAPTER for me to write, because I love so deeply my Rochester and I have loved other animals in the past who have died. Nevertheless, it is a subject that must be mentioned and discussed, because so many humans love their animal companions. Those who do not share their lives with animals or have never thought much about the death of one, perhaps can also be helped in this chapter.

To most humans who love an animal and have shared their daily lives with a beloved one, when death comes to this companion, it is as crushing and heartbreaking as if a human had died. To those who have no animals, this may seem absolutely incredible, and they may even think it wrong. It is not. An animal gives utter love and devotion day in and day out, whereas often humans fail us. To one especially who lives alone with an animal companion, and they belong to each other exclusively, this is even more tragic to the human who is left alone. I am not saying that this death is more devastating than any other—though to some it may be, just that the human involved may need considerable help and consolation. But any death of an animal is unbearable to one who deeply loves their beloved companion.

When anyone remarks to one who has lost an animal friend, "You can always get another one," or "It was only a pet," the speaker is indeed showing no understanding and will certainly add additional pain to the bereaved person. Animal owners often are looked upon as completely strange if they are in grief over their loss. Yet the same people who thus add pain would probably have much compassion if the loss were one of a human family member or friend. In our society, grief over an animal is often unacceptable behavior, and the people who are suffering have to suppress their grief, feel embarrassment over tears, and often must stay away from friends as much as possible. Unfortunately, to suppress their grief can also prolong it. The animal-human bond is an incredibly strong one and not many understand this unless it has been within one's personal experience or within the life of a close friend or family member. From this moment on, however, if you have not realized all of this before and have been insensitive to others concerning the death of animal friends, please pray that you will no longer treat this lightly or utter words that may sear the heart of the human who is experiencing the loss. I believe any veterinarian would speak these same words, as well as anyone involved with animals in any way.

It is important to know that it is normal to grieve over our animal companions, and it is necessary to surround yourself with other humans who understand and care, who can give emotional support. Avoid human friends who will simply minimize your heartbreak. Taking time to grieve is necessary for anyone suffering a loss.

It is very helpful to talk about your animal friend and to have a listener or listeners. To think upon and share the happy times, the unforgettable moments, the unusual things that bound you together, will aid in the grief process. It is especially helpful to talk with friends who also have experienced the loss of a creature in their lives, for they will best understand and be better able to support, console, and lead you through your grief. Talk about the pain with these people, too—about your animal's last days. This is necessary for your healing.

It may even be necessary to talk with your veterinarian alone, or a counsellor—or perhaps your minister or priest or other religious leader.

Before the long days ahead that will contain your grief, first must come some recognition of the life that is now no longer with you. This can be done in ways of your choosing, but a choice must be made as to whether you will bury your friend or have cremation. And then it is comforting to have a memorial service including a eulogy. The eulogy can be delivered by one person—just a few loving words about the beloved animal—or a poem included or a passage of literature, and always prayers. Perhaps, if the animal belonged to a family, each family member could say a few words and speak of special memories each has. It is best to prepare ahead for the death of your companion, so that when the time comes, even in your deep grief, you will know exactly what you want done. But this is difficult to do, this planning ahead, so often, then, we must make decisions at the very time of the death.

I have shared with you all the details concerning Katie's death and her Christian memorial service; perhaps you might like to reread that section before going on to another subject. We did all that we could to make her service meaningful. We had in our favor a waiting period of several days, because the ground was so cold and frozen in New Hampshire, even though she was buried April 2, 1989 and Spring was near. My husband had to begin her grave slowly, and it took a number of days to dig one that would be proper and deep enough, by the lake. But we will never forget that memorial service; all the articles enclosed with Katie held meaning to all involved, as well as the words and prayers said.

When our first little Cairn Terrier died, we were devastated and sad. We could not do as we did for Katie, because we could not go to New Hampshire then and were in Pennsylvania. My husband learned from the ASPCA that cremation would be done; this was my first encounter with cremation, and it upset me. At that time, I had not been a Catholic very long, and even as a Methodist before, I had not been one of the responsible persons for an animal companion's burial, or aware of the proper way to tenderly care for the body. I could not agree to cremation of our beloved little dog, Lizzie, until I learned it was a Christian way and accepted by the church to which I belonged. A call to my priest gave me comfort and also the assurance that to have Lizzie cremated was an acceptable Christian way—for humans and all God's creatures. This gave me a peace I would not have had if we had merely gone ahead without that phone call. Lizzie was a member of our family for sixteen years, and she deserved all the respect that we could give. When our other two dogs died (Lizzie's daughter and son), we then did exactly the same.

Often our animal companions see us through many major events of our lives, as well as the very ordinary every day living—and a proper memorial service and burial or cremation is an absolute. There are special animal cemeteries—and I have known two families to have their beloved companions buried in cemeteries for humans. My aunt and uncle did this for their beloved wire-haired terrier, Pat, and we have other friends who also did this for their dear little dog. If my precious Rochester and I die at the same time—an accident or otherwise—I previously made it known to my husband and several daughters that I wished him to be buried with me after the service, right on my lap or legs or in my arms, just as he spent a great portion of his life. My family had agreed. This is not strange in the least. Another friend of mine has also made this same request concerning her cats. But more recently I have decided on cremation for us both and burial together here on Higher Ground. I pray Bob will decide the same.

Many people feel they still experience their animal's presence in the home after they are gone. I do not feel this is unusual at all. Many people give a donation at the time of their animal's death to a Humane Society or an Animal Shelter—or continue to donate regularly in their animal's name. Sometimes the name is added on a plaque at such places. People often plant a tree in memorial to their beloved companion or a lovely flowering shrub that makes a permanent live and growing tribute. One could put a little plaque or a marker with a tree or shrub inscribed with your animal's name, the dates of birth and death, or anything else in a loving gesture that an individual might want to include. Often people continue prayers and light candles for their animals. Many keep photo albums and other memory albums for their animal friends while they are alive—and after death these are expanded on and cherished. Always, I am sure, a framed picture of the beloved friend will remain in view in the home. Many write poems in memory of their animals or write stories, as I did for Katie. A poem for her will follow at the end of this chapter, written the morning after her death and upon our arrival in New Hampshire with her precious body.

It was part of my help to myself in my grief to write the poem, and then, some days after her memorial service, to write the story. These were also for my daughter Jessica—to help her, even though it was almost a year before she could read them. Her husband Michael was able to read them sooner—one day in his car, he pulled over and parked with the folder that contained them. He said that as he read, somehow through the screen of his open car roof, some small yellow flowers got through and fell over the pages of the written words about Katie, and he felt the flowers had to do with Katie. The flowers were even yellow, as had been the daffodils enclosed with Katie in the quilt. My daughter still has quiet grief over her beautiful "daughter" Katie, but we know we will see her and be together again one day in Heaven. And in the meantime, all family members can visit her grave when they visit New Hampshire, and it is a lovely spot to have quiet time and prayer. Michael has made a beautiful cross from white birch tree branches and tied the bars together. With "Katie" engraved on the horizontal cross piece, it is a very loving memorial at the head of her fine, mounded, rock-covered grave by the lake. Bob later made a poured-cement headstone with her name and dates—also for two other beloved family dogs who have died since and were treated with the same love and respect—each with a service of prayer.

One other suggestion I would like to add, concerning the death of an animal and your grief, is that you begin to keep a journal about your animal. In this journal you can write memories of the life you shared together—special moments or anything that comes to you that you wish to record. A journal is extremely helpful at particularly sad times, when grief is overwhelming and your emotions are devastated anew. Write down those feeling and get them out on paper. Seeing them there in the written word is like having a part of yourself visible that you can analyze and comfort, and you will better understand the emotions within yourself. Keep your journal regularly—and always use it at very difficult times that come out of the blue. Try to use a bound book, perhaps a color you associate with your animal, or particular flowers in the design that held meaning in your lives, or a design on the cover that is pleasing or significant, that only you understand. If you use just scraps of paper to record your thoughts and memories, they can end up lost or separated. This is true of any form of journal keeping. It is much finer to have a bound book that is easily bought in a book or art store with blank pages and a nice cover of your choice; then everything will be in order and you will have it forever—the sad and the joyful—all of which were and are a part of you and your relationship with your beloved animal.

You may use several journals, filling one after another if you are particularly inclined to write. This is good! Your animal will always be a part of you and be written about in years to come, no matter how many journals you go on to use. You can also write poems in your journal for your friend, or if you cannot, you may see poems or quotations written by others in books or magazines that apply to your dear one—and you can copy them in, to be scattered amongst your own writings and feelings. To keep a journal is healing, and it is a private place to meet your precious animal in thoughts and prayers (you may compose written prayers for him or her) and through your personal writing about him that pours out from your soul. I know this will help you.

After this manuscript was completed, the death of a dear little cat occurred. To assuage his own grief and to help his daughter, to whom the little cat had belonged, my friend Dan wrote a beautiful tribute to their sweet friend and brought it to Bob and me upon completion. We three sat at the kitchen table, and I cried as I read about dear little Misty. Dan's "musings" are a form of journal-keeping for him.

We had last seen Misty with her family some months previous— quietly sunning herself in the garden. She was not well then, and the gentle image of her remained with me and I had kept her in my prayers. Dan would give us frequent reports on her health. She had lovingly impressed me, and she was truly worthy of the love continuously given her by her family, and Dan's written tribute. Farewell, little Misty.

If those of you who have not lost an animal, feel you want to help a friend who has—perhaps as soon as possible you could make your friend a gift of a journal, but thoughtfully asking your friend first what color would be preferred, or if there is something significant that should be a concern for the cover. As a long time journal keeper, I know that if I am not content and at peace with the color and design of the cover of a journal, I will balk at using it and will not keep it regularly. I will have to force myself to write in it, even if I am in deep need of writing. But when the cover is appealing in color and design and holds meaning—it constantly draws me to the journal, and I write much more in it and fill it cover to cover, almost before realizing it.

I have actually filled identical journals repeatedly until the need to use a journal with a specific cover has lessened. I am in the process of that now, for I am writing in an identical journal to two others that I have previously filled these past months. I have had a deep need for this certain color and design in these past months and as a result have done much more writing in depth. And so though it may not seem important—to another—colors and patterns can be important. And in the case of grief, one color might actually be very healing and calming and draw the grieving ones to write, whereas another cover of a different hue might actually make them depressed or feel it has no association with their animal, and therefore they will find it very hard to open and write in—or they may not use it at all. So, unusual as all this may sound, please respect your grieving friend if you intend to give a journal to him or her, and ask of the preferences that would appeal and soothe and attract in cover color and design. If you would like the journal to be a surprise, you could simply ask his/her color preferences for a gift you have in mind, and in the course of the discussion perhaps gently learn if the friend is attracted to floral patterns or plainness—or whatever else you can draw from them at this time. Perhaps it will lighten the spirit of the one to know that you want to please, and he/she will express preferences freely. The anticipation of a surprise gift could even be a small bright spot in your friend's darkness, though no material possession is ever comparable to a beloved life, and it might be even somewhat ignored when you do present it. However, it will be in his/her hands with a *written* note from you to say its purpose—and when he/she is once again alone, they may quietly discover its beauty and read your note and begin to write.

Pray for your grieving friends and encourage them to speak of the beloved ones they have lost. To not be able to embrace their animal— or see them or watch their dear antics or experience their devotion and love—is a pain and suffering beyond belief.

Two poems by John Greenleaf Whittier I find very comforting and often include them in letters of sympathy and Mass cards. They are appropriate to write out in a letter to a friend grieving for an animal companion:

❧

With silence as their benediction
God's angels come
Where in the shadow of a great affliction,
the soul sits dumb.

❧

ANGEL OF PATIENCE

To weary hearts, to mourning homes
God's meekest angel gently comes;

No power has he to banish pain,
Or give us back our lost again;

And yet in tenderest love, our dear
And heavenly Father sends him here.

There's quiet in the angel's glance
There's rest in his still countenance!

He mocks no grief with idle cheer,
Nor wounds with words the mourner's ear;

What ills and woes he may not cure
He kindly trains us to endure.

The Tragedy of Lost Pets

Another form of grief must also be addressed—and that is the tragedy of a lost pet. The ache and torment in one's heart in experiencing this is extra dreadful, because unless there is the miracle of the lost one being found and returned, the pain remains. To go through the weeks and months and years of not knowing where your pet is or what may have befallen him is truly a suffering of a dimension that is difficult to explain.

Little voiceless creatures that are as precious to us as life itself—that share our lives and homes and all we do—suddenly can be gone if precautions are not taken.

If you leave your dogs or cats outside unattended, there is always the risk of their disappearance. They can become lost if they should wander far; they can be stolen, or they can be killed in some way. There are people who spend their time picking up stray animals in their cars, whom they sell to others who are unscrupulous and who in turn may sell them to laboratories for research, cults for satanic worship and torture, and to other cruel people who simply like to torment, torture, and kill for entertainment. I have read of the horrendous things such dear companion animals are used for, but to have listed the ones above is sufficient to make you realize that these dangers exist.

I have told you how my little Rochester came to me, but many times since he came into my life I have wondered how his dear little look-a-like sister fared. I pray that she too went to a loving family who love her as we love Rochester. When I see children at malls with a litter of kittens that their parents have probably told them must have other homes— and I see their careless way of taking care of them there in the mall—I become very upset. These kittens are given out to absolute strangers, who may look respectable, but these same persons may want these free kittens for terrible reasons. And their fate then is in the hands of these children, who do not screen a prospective taker. A person with bad intentions would not tell the truth, even if the children were to ask questions. Their parents should be responsible!

It is most important that your companion always wear a collar and identification tag. Our Rochester's tags contain our phone numbers along with that of our veterinarian's—and Rochester's name and phone numbers are also written in permanent ink neatly on the collar. Even though he is an indoor cat and is never outside (unless travelling in his carrier with us), he wears this collar continuously. It is only removed when I comb and groom him regularly, and then immediately it is put back on. This means he sleeps in it at night also. So easily a little cat or dog can slip out of the house when others come in, and if there is no collar on your companion, you may have lost him forever. With the collar, there is at least hope of a return, but not a guarantee. The simple rule is just to never leave your animals outside unsupervised, chained, tied up alone, or to run free. It has been written in many Animal Rights books that cats are far better off kept indoors. Besides all the terrible things that can happen in regard to loss, they can eat poisonous things or be attacked by an unfriendly dog (though cats and dogs often make wonderful companions, as we have experienced), or tormented by children or adults.

Please, make sure your companions always wear their collars and tags, and never leave them unattended, or you may never see them again. A double protection is that of tag and tattoo. Agents and facilities all over United States exist where one can obtain a tattoo for an animal friend. He can then be registered; a procedure is involved whereby he will be coded by state and given a number.

Of all the dogs or cats that end up in a pound, only a low percentage are given to new homes. Most are either killed or given to laboratories.

If your animal companion at this moment is not wearing identification, I hope that you will take steps immediately to correct this. Actually, a combination of tag and tattoo is best, for if a person has evil intentions, a collar can simply be removed and discarded. Of course, a collar and tag has also been the reason for many happy reunions of companion and owner.

To suffer through the disappearance of a lost beloved companion is truly one of the worst things that can happen to the animal's owner, for the owner must live knowing he will never know how his precious animal is or where he is—or if he is at all. And to have the torture within your soul that he many have died a cruel death is truly a despair that will forever remain. Spare yourselves this terrible agony by taking all precautions, and if there are those reading who do not own companions but have seen companion animals belonging to their friends without collar or tag—then they can be of help to these friends and inform them before they suffer the tragedy of a lost animal.

My hope is that these brief sharings help in some way both those who grieve and those who minister to those who do. And may I add that animals too experience grief; they need help and therapy when their owners or animal companions who share their lives die. This too, is very serious; our animals need support and love when they have suffered the loss of human or animal and are grieving. A death of a beloved friend they have been bonded to can also be detrimental to their health, if they are not aided in some way. Do all that you can to love, console, and be with them.

I will share now the poem written the morning following her death in memory of our dear Katherine Elizabeth Kolb Drakely—our Katie—and also one that I wrote on the first anniversary of her death.

Katherine Elizabeth Kolb Drakely
October 31, 1982 - March 28, 1989
—struck down by a hit-&-run truck—

KATIE

Abruptly you left us
No time for good-bye—
Dear little Katie—
And now our hearts cry.

We miss you, sweet puppy
Companion and friend
We are honored you love us—
And will without end.

Lying now peacefully
At our Lord's feet this day
You will hear in your heart
The love words we say.

Time was not given us
To speak them that night
We were robbed of that privilege
Grief and anger we fight.

But now you will know
How we care and we love—
A million times more—
It is multiplied above.

Your soul will be flooded
You'll feel our embraces—
And deep in your heart,
You'll see all our faces.

But one countenance will shine out
More illuminated and bright
Your Mommy's—sweet Jessica,
Her love's reached new height.

Eternally in Jesus
She will live within you
And she will carry your heart
Until this life is through.

Then one day in Heaven
Towards us you'll bound -
We'll be forever together
On God's Higher Ground.

❧

IN MEMORY
(MARCH 1989 - MARCH 1990)

Beside the still water
Lies a sweet "daughter."
Jessica claimed her as "child"
Precious puppy so mild.

A dear dog of great worth
Who gave joy from her birth.
A companion Jess cherished—
Anguished soul when she perished!

The mound of hard rock—
To the left of the dock,
Signifies Holy site
Under blanket of white.
Our Katie—loved dearly—
We shall ever see clearly!
Now she runs on His Shore—
With our Lord evermore.

In memory of Katie
(Katherine Elizabeth Kolb Drakely)
Resting place by Lake Balch, NH

CHAPTER SIXTEEN

❧

Animals and Heaven

"Yet we have this assurance. Those who belong to God shall live again."
—Isaiah 26:19, Living Bible (The Way)

*F*OR AS LONG AS I CAN REMEMBER, it was assumed by people in my life that animals did not go to Heaven. I cannot say where I first heard this teaching, but I recall hearing it throughout my life. It made me uncomfortable and upset, because I loved animals, and my own personal animals were deeply loved in a special way. As a child, I would look into the faces of my little cats, in wonderment at their beauty, and their love and sweetness to me made it very difficult for me to accept that they would not inhabit Heaven. It was a very hurtful belief to live with while growing up and into adulthood. Only those who love animals truly understand what I am expressing. And if you have an animal companion or companions that share all that you do in a deep way, then to believe that they will not share an afterlife with you and that you will not be reunited one day—is a terrible thing. Just as it would cause others deep remorse and suffering to live with the pain of believing a human loved one would not be in Heaven with them, so would those who dearly love and understand and communicate with their animal companions suffer this same pain also.

Several years ago, I bought a wonderful old book of stories written for children by a Christian Protestant pastor. It was a beautiful volume, filled with words to inspire both children and the parents who would share the book. Before giving it to my oldest daughter June, who is married with children, I read many of the writings. Then suddenly I came to a part in a story where it was told to the child that animals did not go to Heaven. I felt sad thinking of all the children through the years who might have been influenced by those words, which were written approximately in the mid-nineteenth century. Here was I, an adult reading it in the late twentieth century, and it troubled me deeply. But at this reading I had already acquired the conviction that this teaching was wrong, and so I wrote a note within the book concerning this to my daughter and her children, so that their minds would not take these words in the story to heart.

Until others who do not live with and love animal companions on a deep spiritual level experience an animal relationship, they simply cannot understand those who do. And so, I continued through life not really believing that our Lord would not have a place for animals in Heaven, yet not able to find absolute proof. Not many Christians I have spoken with personally concerning this have the belief that I now have. My faith will never be shaken in this now, not once this firm conviction was placed within my soul. I can say only that the conviction came gradually through the years, and each time I would hear another say that animals would not be in Heaven, my conviction grew deeper within that they would. Until one moment, when I simply knew!

I know there are many Christians and others who (like myself in the past) find it painful that they will never see their beloved companions again, because that is what they were taught to believe, or it was a definite feeling that they acquired from many sources. I say to you now, so that you may cast this old belief away: rejoice, that you *will* have your dear animal with you in Heaven!

As I said earlier in this book, it is very difficult to be a Christian who does not believe it is moral to slaughter and torture and hunt and kill animals in any way—and then consume their flesh, for we are not hearing that it is wrong in our Churches. Most pious Christians would find it strange to be presented with statements to the contrary. But as Christians, we are baptized in water and by the Spirit, and we have the Holy Spirit within us as our Paraclete and Advocate and Guide. I believe the Holy Spirit speaks to each of us and convicts us of matters in our own lives and of spiritual matters and concerns in the world, and I believe we must listen to Him. When He impresses things on our soul, we must be attentive—or, if need be, *act*. And there is an inner knowing when this happens to us, that the Holy Spirit is impressing and directing us. Often we are never the same when a Holy thought has made its mark upon our soul, for it can change a belief, alter one's life, cause one to speak out—and yet in all of these leave us with a peace and certainty within. He will not leave doubt, for God is not a God of confusion (1 Corinthians 14:33) but of peace. And so we must listen to what the Holy Spirit is saying to us within—and when He speaks to us, *believe!* And then—do not let anyone thereafter shake our belief in what has been impressed on our soul.

I have had major changes in my life occur in this way. I have recognized the Holy Spirit's voice and calling and I could not doubt! And despite all outward circumstances that would contradict and try to say otherwise, I would know that what I heard within was the directive I must follow. An outstanding example from my life was my calling to be a Catholic when I had been reared in the Methodist Church, married in it, and then with my husband reared our six children in the Methodist Church as we both had been. But there is no explaining the calling I had within to be a Catholic. Only those who have gone through similar transformations can understand. I felt like I was in the wrong body, my soul being pulled with a force to the Catholic Church and a deep longing to obey and follow, and yet I remained in the body that took me to my Methodist Church. Through prayer, which made it possible to follow my inner direction, this miracle truly occurred, and I became a Catholic, yet cherishing always my Methodist roots. For eighteen-and-a-half years, despite much pain and suffering in the first six years of that conversion, I knew without a doubt that I was where Our Lord wanted me, doing what he wanted me to do. This step in my spiritual journey was irrevocable, just as becoming a vegetarian was irrevocable. When one hears the Holy Spirit's voice—and obeys—one cannot go back to what was before.

I share this to emphasize that once I had the inner conviction from the Holy Spirit that animals and all God's creatures do inhabit Heaven with us, then I could never believe otherwise. It was irrevocable! No matter what anyone else may argue, I cannot be shaken on this.

Scriptural Evidence

In scripture it is written:

> *Don't let others spoil your faith or joy with their philosophies, their wrong and shallow answers built on men's thoughts and ideas, instead of on what Christ has said.* —Colossians 2:8, The Living Bible (The Way)

This is a powerful verse to remember always. I would also share with you another verse, previously shared in the chapter on Prayer. It has great meaning for me in many areas of my life, and in the lives of many with whom I have shared. This verse is Hebrews 11:1 and I will again use the Living Bible (The Way), for I feel this paraphrase is incredibly filled with encouragement and hope, compared to other translations:

> *What is faith? It is the confident assurance that something we want is going to happen. It is the certainty that what we hope for is waiting for us, even though we cannot see it up ahead.*

Now you who long to know that your animal companions will share Heaven with you—apply this verse to this longing, and claim it *by faith* right now. That entire chapter of Hebrews 11 speaks of the faith of the men and women of old, and we are to have this same faith in our lives, despite circumstances around us that may indicate otherwise, and despite the words of others who would have us believe as they do and try to shake our faith. If God did all the things that are listed and more, including bringing women's sons back from the dead because these women had the faith that He would, then how could we believe otherwise—that He has not intended our beloved animal companions and creatures of the world that He created to share Heaven with us. Why would a merciful God, who asks us to have faith for all things unseen (reread Hebrews 11:1) and a certainty and an assurance, cut down His own creatures and let their wonderful lives end in nothingness? I can never accept that—nor can other Christians who believe as I do and in a merciful God.

Epicurus and Plutarch held the belief that animals had a high intelligence like humans, and Plutarch—the Roman author—was also a vegetarian, as mentioned in an earlier chapter. He held strong beliefs against eating flesh. Both these men believed animals have the ability to understand the nature of things, give familial love, have goodness of character, and make decisions. Plutarch wrote an essay titled "On Eating Flesh," some of which I have quoted in the chapter concerning vegetarianism. He loved and respected animals. The words by him that follow expand on an earlier quotation. After you have read these words that must sear your own souls, then read carefully again the last line of it all.

> *We eat not lions and wolves by way of revenge, but we let those go and catch the harmless and the tame sort, such as have neither stings nor teeth to bite with, and slay them. . . . But if you will contend that yourself were born to an inclination to such good as you have now a mind to eat, do you then yourself kill what you would eat. But do it yourself, without the help of a chopping-knife, mallet, or axe—as wolves, bears, and lions do, who kill and eat at once. Tend an ox with thy teeth, worry a hog with thy mouth, tear a lamb or a hare in pieces, and fall on and eat it alive as they do. But if thou hadst rather stay until what thou eatest is to become dead, and if thou art loath to force a Soul, out of its body, when then dost thou against nature eat an animate thing?* (quoted in *The Extended Circle*)

I believe his words need no further explanation.

God created man out of the ground, and He created animals and wild birds out of the ground. The New American Catholic Bible uses *"clay of the ground"* (Genesis 2:7) and the Living Bible says *"dust of the ground."* In regard to the animals, the New American Catholic Bible states they were *"formed out of the ground"* and the Living Bible states *"formed from the soil."* Man and animal came from the same substance, and therefore many believe—including myself—that animals therefore must have a soul. The Breath breathed into man was the same Breath breathed into the animals, birds, and other creatures.

Genesis, Chapter 1, Verses 21 and 22, of the New American Catholic Bible, states:

God created the great sea monsters and all kinds of swimming creatures with which the water teems and all kinds of winged birds. God saw how good it was and God blessed them.

In the Living Bible the words are slightly different, saying, "*Great Sea Creatures*" and "*Every sort of fish*" and "*Every kind of bird*" and that "*God looked at them with pleasure,*" but the ending of the verses is the same, the fact that "*God blessed them.*" The Living Bible says "*blessed them all.*" In the dictionary, the word "Blessed" is defined in these ways: "To make Holy," "sanctify," "to invoke divine favor upon," "to honor as Holy," "glorify," and "to confer well-being upon."

This is further proof that animals have a soul—or why would God have blessed them? And it is still further proof that they indeed have a soul, because after He created man and woman, God blessed them also! There is no difference stated or indicated in the Bible concerning the "Blessing." It was the same! "*God created man in his image, in the divine image he created him, male and female he created them. God blessed them. . . .*"

The animals gave God pleasure, for it states this in Verse 24, Chapter 1. In the New American Catholic Bible, it says, "*God saw how good it was*" (after He created the animals), and the Living Bible says, "*And God was pleased with what he had done.*" Actually, animals were created to be the companions of Adam, and you can read this in your own Bibles in Genesis 2:18. That animals give pleasure and love and help is evident today, as it has been since Creation. Animals give unconditional love to their human companions, and in the case of children they teach them many things—above all to be kind to all living creatures. Children can learn to be responsible in caring for their companions and learn to be faithful friends to the dear animals that give to the children their own faithfulness. In the lives of the elderly, an animal companion can be a comfort beyond compare to share the days and nights with and to give the elderly the desire to live and to care for their beloved companions. An animal companion prevents loneliness, for all who love and live with animals talk to the animals and share their activities in the home with them, and most confide in them too. It is known that an animal presence in our life can help to lower blood pressure, just in the stroking and petting of a purring cat in one's lap or a dog there or by our side. Will not these blessed creatures (blessed by God) be rewarded in Heaven and share our lives there? Yes, they will!

In the account of the serpent, Geneses 3:1 states, *"Now the serpent was the most cunning of all the creatures that God had made."* The Living Bible says, *"the craftiest."* God created the serpent this way, which is a human trait. "Crafty" also means, as stated in the dictionary (as well as "cunning"), "skilled in deception" and "shrewd." All of these are traits of humans. Eve also carries on a conversation with the serpent, as if he were a human like herself. It seems altogether natural, and she is not in the least frightened or horrified that the serpent can speak. All of this can be read in your Bible and also in Genesis 3:13, where Eve is confronted by God as to why she and Adam ate the fruit, and she answers, *"The serpent tricked me."* Following this, the snake, an animal, shares the blame and the punishment from God. It had the ability to know and choose right from wrong—another proof that animals have souls.

Read now in your Bibles, Genesis 3:14–17, to see the punishments of Adam, Eve, and the serpent. One can only conclude after reading this, no matter what translation of the Bible one uses, that they were treated equally. God considered the serpent equal to Adam and Eve; otherwise, why was it punished? All had sinned, and therefore all were punished. If the animal did not have a soul, why did God punish it?

So many other scripture verses prove God loved the animals and gave them souls. He even gave the same promise to the animals that He gave to Noah concerning never again destroying the earth with a flood—and He sent and sealed His promise with the rainbow, which has been seen from that day forward. His words in scripture concerning the promise are found in Genesis 9:8–11, but I will just write a portion of this:

> God said to Noah and to his sons with him, *"See I am now establishing my covenant with you and your descendants after you, and with every living creature that was with you."* (The Living Bible says, *"And the animals you brought with you."*)

He then names all the animals and birds, both wild and tame, that were there and came out of the ark. If the animals were not blessed and loved by Him, why did He make sure that they went along with Noah on the ark?

All through scripture we read how the animals are dependent on God, and the birds fly to where He has told them to go, and they return. If these were only instincts, as many would argue, and not a form of obedience and reliance on God, then how can one explain this scripture verse of Jeremiah 8:7:

> Even the stork in the air knows its season;
> Turtle dove, swallow, and thrush observe their time of return.
> But my people do not know the ordinance of the Lord.

That was the New American Catholic translation. The ending is even more powerful in the Living Bible:

> They all return at God's appointed time each year, but not my people! They don't accept the laws of God!

One has to interpret that God is displeased with the humans and that the animals obey Him in a far better way than His people obey Him.

Another verse I discovered a long time ago in relation to my believing that animals have souls and go to Heaven is one that proves this point without a doubt. This verse is Jeremiah 9:10 (Living Bible):

> Sobbing and weeping, I point to their mountains and pastures, for now they are desolate, without a living soul. Gone is the lowing of cattle, gone the birds and wild animals. All have fled.

Jeremiah is distraught because all the living souls have fled, and he names the animals, proving most emphatically that they also have souls.

Perhaps this verse was not familiar to everyone, for I have to admit it did not make itself known to me in such a powerful way until I began searching the scriptures more deeply for proof that animals do go to Heaven.

However, there are other verses that most everyone has heard at some time or other, or read for themselves in scripture, or even seen portions of on Christmas cards, with a lion and a lamb pictured together lying down in peace. This scripture can be found in Isaiah 11:6, and no one can deny upon reading it that animals will be with us. They will be on the new earth or in Heaven. This verse begins, *"In that day the wolf and the lamb will lie together, and the leopard and the goat at peace."* The rest you may read in your own Bibles, as well as Isaiah 65:25. When scripture refers to *"in that day,"* we know it is referring to Heaven.

The verse Isaiah 65:25 is wonderful proof that the animals will be there in Heaven with us. There simply can be no denying this!

However, yet another verse supports this; linked with all these others, one has to believe. Hosea 2:20 states, in the New American Catholic translation:

> *I will make a covenant for them on that day, with the beasts of the field, with the birds of the air, and with the things that crawl on the ground. Bow and sword and war I will destroy from the land, and I will let them take their rest in security.*

The Living Bible says it in a slightly different way:

> *At that time I will make a treaty between you and the wild animals, birds and snakes not to fear each other anymore; and I will destroy all weapons and all wars will end.*

There is also the verse in Revelation where there is the amazing picture, the Apostle John's vision, where Jesus and the armies of Heaven come riding on white horses.

So many other things can be considered that will help you to know that your beloved animals will share Heaven with you. First of all, God created the animals, made them in harmony with the universe, and said they were good. Not only that, but He created them for Himself. Scripture supports this also. In the story of creation, we can see the high regard God has for the animals, for their creation immediately followed man's, and they were made out of the same ground as man. I believe animals have a divine purpose in the universe, since God often chose them to be messengers—His own personal ambassadors. In the Old

Testament, the ones I can remember are the dove and the donkey. The dove brought the news to Noah, and God spoke through Baalam's donkey. Also animals inspire others and cause a deep love for God. I know this by the way that love and prayers well up in me when I look at my Rochester. I am continually grateful for this little being in my life. David in the Psalms praised God when he observed and beheld the beasts and the fowl.

I know others will think of other reasons why Our Lord has made provision for animals to be in Heaven with us, besides what I have shared here.

That Quail, Robert *and Other Stories*

Remarkable accounts of animals can be found in books written by people who lived with them or knew them intimately. Two such books are *Born Free* and *Rascal*, but there are many others. If you have never read the true story, *That Quail, Robert* (a best-seller) by Margaret A. Stanger, I suggest you try to obtain it. Animal lovers will cherish this story, and doubters or those not inclined toward animals will surely be amazed. It is a beautiful account of the mysteries of a dear little bird who lived a happy life for four years at a Cape Cod home. It has been described as captivating, charming, incredible, and poignant. I agree—for it touched my heart, and I loved meeting the sweet little bird who loved humans so. Robert was hatched by the warmth of a boudoir lamp, born on a kitchen countertop, and became a cherished member of its adopted family. One can never forget this book, and it only emphasizes all that I am saying in this chapter.

In that book, two other books are mentioned, whose authors tell of the intelligence of birds and how in specific instances they have adapted to human environment with much love and response to the humans. One mentioned is Sally Carrigher, author of *Wild Heritage*, who attributes to certain animals and birds the ability to make decisions, to feel and show affection, to play, and to plan. She even goes so far as to suggest that some of them recognize property rights, fair play, and so on. These conclusions are reached by others who are also close to animals and live and work with them. The author of *That Quail, Robert* had seen similar things concerning the quail, particularly after observing an incident involving a bevy of fourteen.

The Sensitivity of Chimps

Dr. Christian Barnard, the well-known heart specialist, relates an incident concerning two male chimps from a primate colony in Holland, who lived next to each other in separate cages for several months before he used one as a donor. He states:

> When we put him to sleep in his cage in preparation for the operation, he chattered and cried incessantly. We attached no significance to this, but it must have made a great impression on his companion, for when we removed the body to the operating room, the other chimp wept bitterly and was inconsolable for days. The incident made a deep impression on me. I vowed never again to experiment with such sensitive creatures. (This was quoted in *The Extended Circle*, the original being printed in *Good Life Good Death*.)

Animals and birds do have human traits. They feel and despair, they mourn their human companions and animal companions, and they are all that I have shared here in these quotations from the Bible and other sources. How can one not believe that they do not have souls and will not go to Heaven? It is proven again and again. And always, those who live with animal companions know their intelligence and emotions and their unconditional love. Their company often proves finer than that of humans. Their comfort is incomparable!

More Scriptural Evidence

There are other wonderful verses of scripture that prove animals truly will be in Heaven with us. These may be found in Romans 8:19 and 22 (Living Bible):

> For all creation is waiting patiently and hopefully for that future day when God will resurrect his children. . . . For we know that even the things of nature, like animals and plants, suffer in sickness and death as they await this great event.

Why would God include the plants and animals in His Promise, if He was not going to take them to Heaven? They suffer as we do, and therefore He includes them. Think about this verse and reread it. If the animals (and plants) were not going to be part of this great event, why are they waiting for it? In fact, how could they even know about it, if they had not already been promised that it was to include them?

And now I have one other amazing scripture verse to share with you that I do not recall reading previously myself (although I must have in reading the Bible through), which I came across in a remarkable book called *Kinship with All Life*, by J. Allen Boone. Again, like *That Quail, Robert*, you will never forget this book. The scripture I wish to share is Job 12:1-10 (New American Catholic Version):

> *But now ask the beasts to teach you and the birds of the air to tell you. Or the reptiles on earth to instruct you, and the fish of the sea to inform you. Which of these does not know that the hand of God has done this? In his hand is the soul of every living thing, and the life breath of all mankind.*

How can one deny that living creatures do not have souls after reading this scripture? And what is even more amazing is that it instructs us to go to these living creatures for our instruction! In the chapter in which this scripture appears in *Kinship With All Life*, the author tells of two tribal chiefs, one in America and one in Arabia, living thousands of miles apart, yet he states:

> *They share a common vision and move in almost precisely the same mental, spiritual, and physical rhythms. Their lives are held together by the same golden thread.*

Each of these chiefs shared with their animals (ponies, horses, and camels) only the best—and their most gracious thinking. They gave them a high mental and spiritual rating that equaled their own, attributed divine qualities to them, and regarded them as "celestial creatures," and constantly paid tribute to them. Both chiefs —the American Indian and the Bedouin chief of the Arabian Desert—said their thinking expressed genuineness, sincerity, admiration, appreciation, respect, humility, unselfishness, sympathy, and a desire to share their best with their animals.

The Bedouin used his prayer rug by his animal and prayed and talked to him—reading the finest literature and the Koran. He would pray with his animal or animals. This was also true of the American Indian — though he would do all of this within his own tradition. They moved with their animals as if they were rational fellow beings in everything they did. These men did as they were inspired to do and established mental contact with any animal or living thing they met. They believed God breathed wisdom through all living things, making all things persons and brothers. They treated their animals like kin. As the author points out, this was not original with these two chiefs, for Job had also recommended and described this same practice centuries before. The incredible wonder of it all is that neither of these two chiefs had ever heard of Job or read the Bible, yet, though they lived great distances from each other, they were actually following Job's advice. Within their own spirits they were led indeed to go to *"the very beasts"* and *"the birds of the air"* and *"the reptiles"* for guidance, wisdom, and reassurance concerning *"the hand of God"* (new American Catholic Bible) and *"the Eternal's Ways"* (Moffat translation).

Nothing I can say now can add to the utter wonder of all this I've related. Now you must think upon it. Only one conclusion can be reached concerning our animals.

And, knowing that our animals respond to love and attention and kindness and respect and unselfishness and sincerity, we know they are capable of thinking and appreciating all of this and responding. I have related so many personal experiences with Rochester in the earlier chapters of this book to prove all that a little animal is capable of. I know with a certainty that my Rochester responds to all of these qualities and most certainly to prayer. I do talk to him in the ways these chiefs have spoken of, and I do respect him and have continuous mental contact with him. I do treat him as a little person (as I have shared), and just as I would wish to be treated. And he is with me frequently during the day and always at night when I pray. At those times he is always included in those prayers, with prayers for his life and well-being, and each night before I sleep, I bless his forehead with the sign of the cross (as I stated previously), just as I have always blessed the foreheads of my six children. In the quietness of the night, sometimes I read to him softly aloud—mostly poetry.

Forgiveness and Our Animals

Our animals are loyal and faithful to us, they "stand watch" in sickness, and they defend us. They are capable of immense love and oh, how important love is to God. He sees this love in our companions. He also stresses forgiveness. Do not our animals forgive us if we have made a mistake and hurt them? They truly do, and they return to loving us in full measure and then some. I am in awe of the love that is given to me by Rochester.

Animals also seek to be forgiven, and I have experienced this through Rochester and also in a very dramatic instance concerning Katie. My daughter had just purchased a pair of new shoes that were still in the box. Jessica was at school and Katie was going through the stage of chewing everything she found, because she was young. On this particular day, I walked into the upstairs hallway to find Katie with one of Jessica's new shoes. It was already so well chewed that it could never be worn. I had never scolded Katie. I felt it was Jessica's duty, and Katie should know Jessica's authority. But on this occasion I truly scolded her, because I knew Jessica had paid a lot for her new shoes and would be upset that they could never be used. I raised my voice and looked right at her and directed her to go downstairs. She knew her "Grandmom" was most unhappy with her!

I calmed down and went about my work. At least three hours had passed when I went into the bedroom to sit and relax and read. I had not been there long when I heard a small noise. It was Katie. She was coming from the hall and into my room on her tummy—actually crawling along with head bowed. I could not believe this and sat quietly waiting to see what she would do. She crawled over to my feet and then very gradually began to actually crawl up the front of me with her front feet, until her paws rested up near my shoulders. With head bowed and big brown eyes looking upward into my eyes, she was literally begging my forgiveness for what she had done. I sat in awe—spellbound! I felt as though I were in another world, to have this lovely creature come to me in this way. I cried and hugged her and got her head all wet and kissed her forehead and assured her by my love and my words to her that I did forgive her and that it was all forgotten. Slowly she became freed, and I began to act joyful then, to show her how happy I was with her—and we played and rough-housed a bit, right then and there, and the two of us then headed downstairs. Katie was washed clean and forgiven! I will never forget this incident or her eyes looking into mine seeking forgiveness and feeling their sad impact on me. This was a young puppy who did not go downstairs after being scolded, immediately to forget and enjoy life. No! She had suffered and three hours later was still feeling so much remorse that she had crawled to me to ask that I forgive her. Tell me how she could possibly have experienced such deep pain and three long hours later come to me begging that we reconcile—if she did not have a soul and understand that she needed to be forgiven? I feel privileged to have been a part of this incident and of her entire life.

Books Dedicated to Animal Companions

So many men and women dedicate books to their animal companions or write books about them—treating them as they would human friends. I am one of these, but one well-known author is James Herriot, the Yorkshire veterinarian who dedicated his *All Things Wise and Wonderful,* one of a series of books by this author:

> *To my dogs*
> *Hector and Dan*
> *Faithful companions in the daily round.*

Perhaps his other books are also dedicated to his animals.

Ingrid Newkirk, author of the recent book, *Save the Animals,* and National Director of People for the Ethical Treatment of Animals, has dedicated her book:

> *To the memory of Ms. Bea, an old mixed-breed dog who died in 1986. The world had not treated her kindly in puppyhood, and when she left, a piece of my heart went with her. I now know that every animal is someone's Ms. Bea or simply a Ms. Bea no one got to know.*

How beautiful! One knows by reading that the love this woman and her companion shared was exceptional.

Books by Cleveland Amory, founder and president of "Italics," have touched millions of hearts through stories about his life with his cat "Polar Bear." He has authored *The Cat Who Came for Christmas, The Cat and the Curmudgeon*, and *The Best Cat Ever*. Why do people from various walks of life feel they need to give such dignity and love to their animals by immortalizing them in "dedications" and in entire books? It is because they have found them worthy and filled with the traits that ennoble and enrich our lives! And this so because our dear companions have souls, and they truly will share Heaven with us.

A beautiful quotation by a priest, Jean Gautier (1875-1964), about his dog, punctuates how an animal's life and death can truly be a part of us, just as any human's:

> I wrote this book because I wished to fix the memory of my dog Uni, whose qualities were great and whose death caused and still causes me much sorrow: I wished also to call people's attention to unfortunate dogs, and my final object has been to show the clergy of my country, who have little understanding of things that concern animals, that man is not a centre but that all creation—man, animals, plants—is oriented towards God and that, in fact, we are all of a piece (Solidaires) (from "A Priest and His Dog").

The well-known Christian writer and theologian, C. S. Lewis, has also expressed opinions on this very subject of animals in Heaven. I will share only a small segment of his long passage concerning this.

The Resurrection of the Animals (the writer speaks first of paradisal man with the creatures):

> Wholly commanding himself, he commanded all lower lives with which he came into contact. Even now we meet rare individuals who have a mysterious power of taming beasts. This power the Paradisal man enjoyed in eminence, the old picture of the brutes sporting before Adam and fawning upon him may not be wholly symbolical. Even now more animals than you might expect are ready to adore man if they are given a reasonable opportunity: for man was made to be the priest and even, in one sense, the Christ, of the animals—the mediator through whom they apprehend so much of the Divine splendour.
>
> Atheists naturally regard the coexistence of man and the other animals as a mere contingent result of interacting biological interference of one species with another. The "real" or "natural" animal to them is the

wild one, but the tame animal is an artificial or unnatural thing. But a Christian must not think so. Man was appointed by God to have dominion over the beasts, and everything a man does to an animal is either a lawful exercise, or a sacrilegious abuse, of an authority by divine right. The tame animal is therefore, in the deepest sense, the only "natural" animal—the only one we see occupying the place it was made to occupy, and it is on the tame animal that we must base all our doctrine of beasts. Now it will be seen that, in so far as the tame animal has a real self or personality, it owes this almost entirely to its master. If a good sheepdog seems "almost human," that is because a good shepherd has made it so.

It seems to me possible that certain animals may have an immortality, not in themselves, but in the immortality of their masters. If you ask, concerning an animal thus raised as a member of the whole body of the homestead, where its personal deity resides, I answer, "Where its identity always did reside even in the earthly life—in its relation to the Body and especially to the master who is head of that Body." In other words the man will know his dog; the dog, will know its master and, in knowing him, will be itself. (quoted in *A Book of Comfort: A Treasury of Prose and Poetry* —Elizabeth Goudge)

My prayer is that those who were questioning and hoping and needing reassurance that their beloved companions will indeed be with them in Heaven, are now comforted by all that has been shared and written in this chapter, and that they have peace of heart now and forever in this regard—and that those who did not believe can now also find this truth absorbed as a part of their beliefs also.

A tender little article appeared in a recent *Catholic Standard and Times*, the Diocese Newspaper of the Philadelphia Area, and it told of an English Atonement friar who was able to get an assortment of famous people to contribute their thoughts for a book on Heaven—from Princess Anne to Mother Teresa, and from Archbishop Desmond Tutu to evangelist Billy Graham. The friar, Father Michael Seed, a chaplain at London's Westminster Cathedral and advisor on ecumenism to George Cardinal Basil Hume, was asked to write a book on Heaven but did not have enough ideas of his own. He sent out many letters explaining his project, and many prominent people were intrigued and willing to respond. The article stated that he was seeking now to sell the letters at an auction and would use the proceeds for sheltering the homeless—with royalties to his order. The book was featured at the annual international book fair in Frankfurt, Germany, and he expected soon that negotiations would be made for a U.S. publisher to bring out an American edition.

Father Seed dedicated the book to Mother Teresa, and respondents included the Dalai Lama, Lord Immanuel Jakobovits, and other representatives of non-Christian and even non-religious traditions.

The touching aspect of it all to me was that after all these famous people from all backgrounds submitted their personal beliefs about Heaven, the title of this profound book was gleaned in an unusual way. When movie star Sean Connery wrote to Father Seed that he was too busy on his next movie to contribute, he closed by saying, "I will see you in Heaven." Father Seed joined that with the contribution of an eight-year-old boy and titled the book, *I Will See You in Heaven—Where Animals Don't Bite*.

Through the thoughts of innocent children we are often given deep wisdom. In Isaiah it states, *"and a little child shall lead them."* I say Amen to the declaration of this title.

Bearers of the Spirit

I would like to include one other very special testimony, before concluding this chapter, from a very close spiritual friend. Daniel Deane, a lawyer of Wyncote, Pennsylvania, told me of a conversation he had with the veterinarian who cared for his dog. It was so reassuring, and on this very subject, that I asked him to put in writing all that he had shared with me. The testimony that follows is one that I pray will confirm and emphasize all that I have written here from my heart, from the scriptures, and from the words and thoughts of others who love and care and know about animals and believe as I do.

Many years ago I was with Dr. VanSant, a veterinarian, driving to a meeting with the dean of the University of Pennsylvania. At the time I had a German shepherd bitch that I adored, and a cat. I asked Dr. VanSant how certain animals could appear to be so intelligent when we knew that their brains were far less developed than those of men or even certain other animals. The doctor said that animals that were closely associated with men, such as horses, or who lived with them, like dogs and cats, frequently seemed to vicariously incorporate some of the intelligence of their owners and become mentally-enhanced animals, despite their limited brains.

I later remembered my summers as a young boy on a farm, when I would be out in the fields working with a pair of draft horses for hours on end, cultivating corn or mowing or raking hay, talking to the horses to relieve my boredom. It seemed to me that over a period of time, a favorite mule or horse would seem to respond to my overtures of friendship, and we would develop some sort of a relationship that was far more than merely a boy with a beast. Consider the cowboy alone on the range with only his horse for company. My relationship with Heidi, my German shepherd, was far closer of course, than any relationship I had ever had with the other animals, but only in the matter of degree, not in kind.

It should be remembered that biologically man is an animal; has a body, members, and internal organs like an animal; and behaves like an animal in fulfilling his physical needs. What makes man different from an animal is the fact that he has a spirit: that part of him created in the image of God and which makes him a person. When a man has a close relationship with an animal, maybe, in some way, that animal assimilates some of the man's spirit and becomes more than merely an animal—an enhanced animal, with a piece of the man's spirit. If this were so, then we would be participating in God's ongoing creation as bearers of the spirit in some small way to animals.

In Genesis 1, man was given dominion over the animals. In Genesis 2, God said, "It is not good that the man should be alone," so God "formed every beast of the field and every bird of the air and brought them to the man to see what he would call them," and the animals were to be helpers for man. (There was not found a helper "fit" for man, however, so God made a woman out of the man's rib.) The relationship of men to animals later changed, when in Genesis 9, after the return to dry land, God told Noah and his sons that the fear of them would be upon every *animal and allowed them meat for food, just as He had previously given them the green plants, but He forbade blood. From this we can reasonably infer that man once had a close and familiar relationship with animals.*

Most of us tend to anthropomorphize our favorite animals or pets and attribute our human qualities to them. Probably the greatest anthropomorphizer of all time was St. Francis of Assisi. Is it not possible that these same animals might be imbued with some instinct, then, to adopt in some way and to some degree the human qualities that man attributes to them? I tend to believe that one day, in God's Heaven, we will again hug our cherished pet animals, ride on the backs of winged horses, and walk up to both the lamb and the lion and playfully scratch them behind their ears. —Daniel T. Deane, Jr.

May Dan's thoughts and words be added here to bring further faith and hope to all those who know and believe that they will be in Heaven with their beloved animal companions.

What is faith? It is the confident assurance that something we want is going to happen. It is the certainty that what we hope for is waiting for us, even though we cannot see it up ahead. —Hebrews 11:1 *(Living Bible)*

CHAPTER SEVENTEEN

❖

Christian Thoughts on Animal Rights

"If we cut up beasts simply because they cannot prevent us and because we are backing our own side in the struggle for existence, it is only logical to cut up imbeciles, criminals, enemies, or capitalists for the same reason."
—C. S. Lewis

As I BEGAN TO COLLECT QUOTATIONS by Christians concerning the protection and saving of God's creatures from slaughter, torture, vivisection, experimentation, and from being hunted, I became very disheartened. It was no easy work to find statements from Christians. In comparison to statements by those of other religions and by those whose religion was not stated but who were humane individuals active in the Animal Rights Movement or in other similar societies, the statements by Christians were in a tiny minority. I realize many Christians are involved in these active groups, doing their work of love, without speaking publicly about it. Nevertheless, there simply is not an abundance of support by Christians in the written word that can witness to all peoples of the world concerning God's Creatures and these terrible assaults upon their existence. One knows, after reading about these issues, where other religions stand. One knows the religions that protest killing and give compassion to all life—not just to human life. That there is so much indifference and division about it amongst Christians is very distressing. It is sad to know that Christians have the reputation for not caring and that because the Bible has stated that we have dominion over the animals that they then may be killed, eaten, tortured, and all else that goes along with these horrendous acts. There is little evidence that Christians in general believe that God's creatures were entrusted into our care and were meant to share the earth with us and to live out their natural lives, as humans may, if not beset by the similar violence that humans put upon the creatures.

An inner moral law should speak to the conscience of each Christian—that God's creatures should not be slaughtered, hunted, or their flesh be eaten and worn for the pleasures of man, when God has provided alternatives of worth in the world, in place of destroying sentient life. Again I point you to the book *Animal Liberation,* by Peter Singer, for an in-depth study of the word "dominion" and all things related to this concept. I am certain that if nothing else strikes the conscience of readers, the photographs alone in this book would cause any God-fearing believer to pause and search his own soul and experience a confrontation within. I will not attempt such a discussion or coverage in this book when one such as Mr. Singer's exists, along with the quotations on these matters in *The Extended Circle,* edited by Jon Wynne Tyson.

The Views of Pope John Paul II

I will, however, include a quotation by Pope John Paul II that is in the chapter called "Man's Dominion" in *Animal Liberation,* to show that a change is taking place and that the Pope has urged that human development should include *"respect for the beings which constitute the natural world."* It is not an outright decree to stop the killing, as other religions have made and live by, but it was made as recently as 1988 and showed that there was a definite change, in the opposite direction, from a statement made by the Catholic Church in the second half of the twentieth century, based on statements by Aquinas. Pope John Paul II also added:

> *The dominion granted to man by the Creator is not an absolute power, nor can one speak of a freedom to "use and misuse" or to dispose*

of things as one pleases. . . . When it comes to the natural world, we are subject not only to biological laws, but also to moral ones, which cannot be violated with impunity." (Encyclical Solicitudeo Rei Socialis, "On Social Concerns" from *Animal Liberation*, Peter Singer)

St. Thomas Aquinas, on the other hand, did not believe it was a sin to be cruel to animals, and he stated we must not show any charity to them either. He believed it did not matter how man behaved toward animals, and the statement made by the church in the second part of the twentieth century was based on Aquinas's thoughts and quoted from his statements.

Though I consider it a miracle through prayer that I am a Catholic and a blessing of the highest magnitude, I cannot agree with any part of Aquinas' views and simply am in shock that such a great thinker and theologian could come to such conclusions without his conscience being stricken. There have, fortunately, been many humane Catholics—St. Francis of Assisi the exception most remembered. The wonderful St. Martin de Torres of Lima, Peru, is another remembered for his love, care, and protection of animals and for his many other Holy attributes. Also, many humane Catholics in the world today would not harm animals or consume them. I have also mentioned previously various other Saints in the past who spoke out in defense of the animals.

The Example of Albert Schweitzer

This chapter would not be complete without mention of Albert Schweitzer, one of the twentieth century's greatest men. His book, *Out of My Life and Thought*, should be read by every Christian and non-Christian also. To give him only a small part of a chapter when he deserves an entire book is sad, but one must really read Schweitzer's book rather than all I could relate about him here. Dr. Schweitzer speaks of Reverence for Life and lived by this principle. He states:

> *The idea of Reverence for Life offers itself as the realistic answer to the realistic question of how man and the world are related to each other.*

He goes on to state, powerfully:

As a being in an active relation to the world, he comes into a spiritual relation with it by not living for himself alone, but feeling himself one with all life that comes within his reach. . . . Let a man once begin to think about the mystery of his life and the links which connect him with the life that fills the world, and he cannot but bring to bear upon his own life and all other life that comes within his reach the principle of Reverence for Life, and manifest this principal by ethical affirmation of life. Existence will thereby become harder for him in every respect than it would if he lived for himself, but at the same time it will be richer, more beautiful, and happier. It will become, instead of mere living, a real experience of life. . . . The ethic of Reverence for Life is the ethic of Love widened into universality. It is the ethic of Jesus, now recognized as a logical consequence of thought.

There are other words we must hear from Schweitzer in this chapter, for these words are from a man whose Lord was Jesus Christ.

The ethic of Reverence for Life is found particularly strange because it establishes no dividing line between higher and lower, between more valuable and less valuable life. . . . To the man who is truly ethical, all life is sacred, including that which from the human point of view seems lower in the scale.

Much more follows these writings of his, just in one chapter alone of his book, but I will attempt only to share what spoke to my own heart in a powerful way—and suggest once more that you read his wonderful book on your own. He states:

Devoted as I was from boyhood to the cause of the protection of animal life, it is a special joy to me that the universal ethic of Reverence for Life shows the sympathy with animals, which is so often represented as sentimentality, to be a duty which no thinking man can escape. When will the time come when public opinion will tolerate no longer any popular amusements which depend on the ill-treatment of animals!

And then, to conclude these quotations of Dr. Schweitzer's, I include:

Christianity has need of thought that it may come to the consciousness of its real self. For centuries it treasured the great commandment of love and mercy as traditional truth without recognizing it as a reason for opposing slavery, witch burning, torture, and all the other ancient and medieval forms of inhumanity. . . . What Christianity needs is that it shall be filled to overflowing with the spirit of Jesus, and in the strength of that shall spiritualize itself into a living religion of inwardness and love. Only as such can it become the leaven in the spiritual life of mankind. Because I am devoted to Christianity in deep affection, I am trying to serve it with loyalty and sincerity.

In closing this portion on Dr. Schweitzer, I would like to include the following journal entries of Dr. Emory Ross of the Foreign Missions Conference, who was the secretary-treasurer of The Albert Schweitzer Fellowship in America at the time he and his wife visited the Schweitzers at Lambarene in August 1946. They had arrived after dark, in the blackness of night, and were greeted enthusiastically by Dr. Schweitzer. Dr. Ross writes:

Thus it was that we met this man, whom we have always considered great, but whose true greatness was to grow and impress itself upon us in the few days we were privileged to spend in his presence, and in the presence of the work which he has hewn out of one of Africa's most jungled forests.

But it is this next entry in his journal that will show that Albert Schweitzer truly lived by the principle of Reverence for Life:

At 7:30 the bell rang for breakfast, and we came out into the strange world which darkness had covered, as we came into it the night before. And what a world! Under the house and around it is a veritable menagerie: chickens, geese, turkeys, cats, dogs, goats, antelope, birds, etc. A pelican is a faithful devotee and, although Mrs. Schweitzer insists on its going off to sleep, still it comes back daily to mingle with the congregation of birds and beasts which have gathered around Dr. Schweitzer. He is truly another St. Francis of Assisi. Nights, as he writes on his philosophy, a yellow and white cat, which he saved as a kitten, curls up around his lamp. As he talked to us of Karl Barth and other philosophers, he would occasionally stroke the cat's head tenderly and speak to it or of it.

In another book written about Dr. Schweitzer, by Charles R. Jay, this same cat was mentioned and seen in a picture with the Doctor. The cat was on his desk as he worked and wrote prescriptions. Under the picture it was noted that "Sizi the cat often falls to sleep on the Doctor's left arm. The Doctor continues to write with his right hand, but he will not move his left arm while the cat is asleep on it."

Dr. Schweitzer remained at Lambarene without vacation for nearly ten years. Truly, this is a great Christian man, one whom we cannot ignore in our spiritual journey to the principle of Reverence for Life. From out of his life and thoughts may we be helped and inspired to live in this humane way, for there is no other way if we are followers of Jesus—for it is an ethic of Love, an imperative of Love.

In the back of this book is an appendix entitled "Passages to Ponder on Our Relationship with Animals." In it, I share with you the thoughts of other Christians that I hope will inspire all readers to search their hearts and become protectors of and voices for all the creatures with whom we share this earth. I suggest that you read each passage very slowly and carefully—returning to them often, even after you have completed the entire book, for each quotation is a meditation.

Though it may seem there are many, you will note as you read that the majority of these fine people are from our past and are no longer alive. Some also are from England and other places. It was difficult to find statements of present-day Christians whose names would be recognized by most people.

Also, and very important, you will find that individuals speak out against the various horrors that beset animals, but very few Christians speak out about the entire scope of horrendous acts done against them. One person may address the despicable practice of vivisection, while another decries hunting or slaughter, but it is a rare Christian in this collection that simply says, "*All of these horrors must be stopped!*"

It becomes more and more evident that a clear and definite statement or creed concerning our fellow creatures who share this earth with us should be prayerfully promoted for consideration, and that all Christian denominations should take part in the creating of it—and then, in one Voice, Christians should tell the world their creed and forever stand by it. *Ahimsa* (harmlessness or nonviolence) is not just for other religions. It should be especially for Christians—who claim to follow the One who is All Love.

I will close this chapter with a powerful statement by a Catholic Christian of this present time, one who has emphasized all I have tried to express and with whom I absolutely agree:

> *I am a Catholic and, consequently, for me there can be no vicarious satisfaction in the thought that a person who has misbehaved cruelly towards animals will pay for it in a future life, when he or she becomes a fox and is hunted by the very pack of which he (or she) was the proud master. It is clear to me, however, that when, if ever, humanity lays aside its suicidal quarrels, and becomes one, the philosophical principle of Buddhism or Hinduism, in their attitude towards animals, must be integrated to the Way, the Truth, and the Life of all mankind.*
>
> *The so-called acceptance of natural cruelty as something over which we should shrug our shoulders is not the view which the purest religious thinkers have taken. To them, cruelty is always cruelty and a hard thing, if not impossible to reconcile with the character of the All-Good.*
>
> *It is our duty as men and women of God's redeemed creation to try not to increase the suffering of the world, but to lessen it.*
>
> —Leslie G. Pine (1907-)

May this speak to the hearts of all Christians.

In loving memory of Sweetpea (Hudson)

CHAPTER EIGHTEEN

❧

Additional Atrocities Against Animals

*"The belief in a supernatural source of evil is not necessary;
men alone are quite capable of every wickedness."*
—Joseph Conrad

WHEN I BEGAN THIS BOOK, I knew I would have to discuss in some way the major issues of experimenting on animals, hunting, vivisection, and other concerns I have already spoken of. This troubled me, because I feel other books by those having done research on these subjects have been written, and what I could contribute would be very little—though my heart is filled with pain over the existence of these horrors. While praying as to how to briefly present these concerns, an article from the *Philadelphia Inquirer* was given to me that appeared October 26, 1990, and it so covered all of these subjects with humane and honorable thinking that I am going to present that article to you, for it also relates what I feel within. I also feel it is a powerful writing from a Christian stance.

I would also like to present a shorter article by a United Methodist woman who has taken a firm stand. This appeared in *The United Methodist Reporter* newspaper at least three to four years ago, and I have kept it—though not saving it because of this book, because I did not know then that I would write one on animals. I saved it to share with others in letters I send out, periodically making copies of it, just as I have

146

of the article by Thomas Donahue. I pray you will read these articles carefully and then make the concerns that are written about, matters of deep prayer.

THE MORAL ARGUMENT FOR SPARING ANIMALS
by Thomas J. Donahue

Concern is growing in American society for the welfare, protection, and rights of animals. Protests have been mounted against killing animals for their fur, hunting animals for sport, and experimenting on animals in the laboratory. A powerful rational argument can be made for respecting animals much more than we currently do.

Every year, tens of millions of animals (including dogs, cats, rabbits, and monkeys) die in often painful laboratory experiments. In many cases, they die not so that we can achieve some major medical break-through, but so that we have one more type of lipstick or one more brand of aftershave. Contrary to the common belief that all or most animal testing is medical in nature, countless animals are tortured and killed daily, so that we can place yet another nonessential item on our already overstuffed shelves.

We also slaughter billions of feeling, sensitive creatures (which we clinically label "livestock" and "poultry") to satisfy our seemingly insatiable appetite for the flesh of dead animals. Often, these animals have short, miserable lives, characterized principally by confinement, stress, and early death—all so that we can dine as we please.

If such things were done to human beings, words like atrocity and genocide would immediately be heard. If such practices would be morally abominable if perpetrated upon humans, they are morally unacceptable when done to animals, unless there is a morally relevant difference in the value of human animals and the value of nonhuman animals.

Many attempts have been made to argue for such a great moral difference in the hope of getting us off the moral hook for what we do to and with animals. Some people contend that, because we are human and animals aren't, we count morally, while they don't. But in the absence of an explanation that specifies why belonging to our species gives us a unique moral status, such a claim seems to be nothing more than arbitrary discrimination in favor of "us" and at the expense of "them." Its parallels with sexism and racism have induced certain thinkers to label such an attitude "speciesism."

Some have pointed to our greater intelligence as the key factor justifying our lethal exploitation of animals to satisfy often trivial desires. However, if the possession of higher order mentality is required in order to deserve moral respect, severely retarded people could conceivably be fair game for exploitation or experimentation by their more intelligent fellow humans.

Surely it is absurd to contend that animals have no rights merely because they lack rational intelligence, since, as should be clear to everyone, it would be absurd to conclude that mentally retarded humans have no rights, due to their similar lack of rational intelligence.

It has also been claimed that we are worth more than animals because we have immortal souls and they don't. This reason is both questionable and irrelevant. First of all, no one knows that such a claim is true. How do you ascertain the presence or the absence of such a soul? Second, even if it were true that we have immortal souls and that other animals don't, how could this make our mortal lives more valuable than those of animals? After all, our mortal lives would not have to persist in order for us to continue to exist, since we would have immortal souls; whereas, for a being without an immortal soul, its mortal life is of paramount importance, since this is its only period of existence. Not having an immortal soul makes one's mortal life more valuable, not less valuable.

Last, it has been contended that God gave us dominion over the entire natural creation, including the animals, and thus that we can treat them as we see fit. Of course, this divine permission is quite unverifiable. Moreover, does it make sense to assume that a supremely merciful God would give us the right to treat animals in a profoundly unmerciful way? Would such a God really go along with the torturing and killing of his sentient creatures, just so that we can consume the latest luxury item, like a "new and improved" bleach? I think not.

Thus, the burgeoning animal-rights movement confronts us with a stark and uncomfortable dilemma: either find a genuine justification for our current practices or abandon them as immoral. The fate of millions of feeling, defenseless, and innocent creatures is hanging in the balance.

—Thomas Donahue teaches philosophy at Mercyhurst College, Erie, Pennsylvania. This column first appeared in the *Christian Science Monitor*. Reprinted with permission.

❧

HERE I STAND: LOVE ETHIC INCLUDES ANIMALS
by Connie Hastings

I'm glad to see the United Methodist Church taking an active part in social and political issues. Now I think it's time for us to address the issue of animal rights.

We seem to be stuck in a prejudice that's similar to other prejudices this country has already come to grips with—against slaves, Irish, Blacks, children, women, and a host of others. Those involve groups of people different from our own.

Now we're being asked to consider the welfare of species other than our own.

Just as with these other prejudices, our prejudice against animals makes us believe their suffering isn't important, that animals don't experience life in the same way we do, and that their behavior is largely instinctive—even that they don't feel pain.

Are these assumptions true? Or have we accepted them without question?

The world has never known such a holocaust of animal suffering as is now taking place in the Western Hemisphere. Billions of animals each year are being raised in the most brutal conditions and slaughtered horribly for food.

Research and testing laboratories are subjecting 100 million of them each year to the most agonizing tortures, most of which are not aimed at curing human disease.

Animals are hunted, trapped, poisoned, and subjected to every conceivable torment by humans for profit and pleasure.

Did you know that:

- *more than half of the mail received by public officials now concerns animal rights?*
- *three laboratories have now been closed because of incontrovertible proof that their experiments were being done in ways that were not only cruel but unsanitary and unscientific?*
- *books are available that would help in your church school's discussion of animal rights? Your local Society for the Prevention*

of Cruelty to Animals or Humane Society can probably obtain copies for you.

Some of the world's greatest thinkers have been advocates of animal rights.

Leonardo DaVinci: "The day will come when men such as I will look upon the murder of animals as they now look upon the murder of men."

Thomas A. Edison: "Until we stop harming all other living beings, we are still savages."

Albert Schweitzer: "To think out in every implication the ethic of love for all creation—this is the difficult task which confronts our age."

Reprinted with permission.

Are We Human or Inhuman?

Through pondering the animals and their plight and suffering at the hands of human beings, it struck me that if the animals could talk to humans, would humans still destroy them and torture them as they do? Not long after that thought, I came across a quotation by Francois Voltaire (in *Princes of Babylon*):

If animals could talk, would we then dare to kill and eat them? How could we then justify such fratricide?

Perhaps this thought has crossed the minds of many who love animals.

Also, during a period in early January when we were back in Pennsylvania and I had to cease writing on this book temporarily, an article appeared in our local paper there that horrified me. A fifty-nine-year-old man had been struck by a hit-and-run driver at an intersection at 7:30 p.m. and another man, realizing that this was "not just a pile of rags lying in the road," stopped to investigate and was almost hit himself as he tried to help the other man. He also told police how he saw young people running out, trying to go through the pockets of the dying man, to rob him, when he arrived. He had to run them off several times.

The "good Samaritan" who had stopped to help said that he was particularly horrified that there were many people standing around on the street corner, laughing and joking about it and using the whole thing to entertain themselves. None had tried to help the man who was struck, though he had been hit by more than one vehicle. He later died in the hospital that same evening, which was my birthday. I have prayed for him frequently at Mass and would have regardless, but I felt somehow responsible to help him spiritually because we shared a day in December.

An officer said a similar thing had happened just weeks before in Philadelphia, when a pedestrian who was struck by a car told police that people were coming out to go through his pockets while he lay there—but no one would help him.

The first incident happened in a suburb of Philadelphia just five minutes' driving time from our home and on the outskirts of Philadelphia. This was not a center city incident, where gangs are about and there is heavier crime. This was a suburb! How can we expect human beings to value animal life and protect the animals from their plights, when fellow human beings are treated in this way by their fellow men? It surely made me see that it could be a very long time before God's creatures are spared by humans. I pray I am wrong.

Here also is a letter sent in to the *Rochester* (New Hampshire) *Courier* that appeared July 30, 1990. May this account strike your heart and perhaps move you to reach out to the animals in some way to stop their suffering in all the various and many ways it exists.

Cruelly Abused

> *To the editor:*
>
> *As administrative assistant for the NHSPCA, I've experienced many things: I've held abused animals in my arms, transported injured wildlife to local veterinarians, witnessed heartwarming acts of compassion, done my best to console a pet owner's grief, and have received the generous donations of the Society supporters.*

Today was a first, however. I went on my first cruelty investigation. A concerned citizen came into our office after finding the body of a dead dog chained to a wire fence set back about 20 feet in the woods off of Rte. 101. He was "blueberrying" and came across its body.

I met an Epping Police Officer and a Fish & Game Conservation Officer and together we set off into the woods. We found the mesh fence, followed it, and after a short distance, a rusted choke chain came into view, attached to the fence. The weathered skeleton of a medium-sized dog lay on the ground, partially covered by leaves and debris. The body had been there for over a year.

This dog was abandoned. This living being was chained and left to die a slow agonizing death, by starvation and dehydration. Chained at such height, it couldn't lie down. The dog was forced to sit, upright, as hunger and dehydration slowly took its life. Its barking most likely was drowned out by the incessant traffic on Rte. 101. When there was no traffic, well, it was such a remote area, no one would have heard his call for help, anyway.

It was a cruel, senseless, and barbaric act, Why? Why, when there were other options that were one hundred times more humane. The simple solution would have been to take the animal to a shelter.

Most likely, we will never know the person that abandoned this poor animal, but the dog knew, and I'm sure, the individual must remember. I know I shall never forget. How many will die like this before we humans become truly humane?

Sincerely,
Helene M. Jones
Administrative Asst.
SPCA, Stratham

My husband and I were just stricken by the cruelty and horrendous act that was committed against this innocent animal. Who could deliberately do such an inhumane thing? One day that person or persons will have to answer to God for what was done to this poor animal. I believe Our Lord, in some way we may never know, ministered to this dog and then held him in his arms when he at last died. He knows when even the tiniest sparrow falls, and surely He was there for this cruelly abused animal. We have thought of this so many times and the horrible suffering the dog experienced at a human's hands.

Choose Cruelty-Free Cosmetics

People should also be aware of cosmetics and personal care items that they buy, to make sure they have not been tested on animals. The Humane Society of the United States has launched a nationwide campaign to promote cosmetics and other personal care products such as these, which they have entitled "The Beautiful Choice." Please look for these products in your natural food stores, beauty salons, and other stores—and purchase products that have not caused suffering to animals. Other individual companies on television often advertise that their products have not been tested on animals. If you care about animals, do not purchase anything until you are certain no animal has been caused pain so that you may feel personally refreshed and beautiful. Know what you are buying!

Fur Coats—Symbols of Suffering

To wear real furs now is also very unfashionable and simply shows that you have an indifference toward the animals that suffer to supply them. Recently, Bob Barker, long time game show host of "The Price is Right" and of the previous show "Truth or Consequences" (1956–1974) has taken a stand that could certainly hurt his popularity, but he has not shunned the controversy. He ended his long-time role as emcee of the annual CBS Specials, such as the Rose Bowl Parade, the Miss Universe Pageant, and the Miss USA Pageant, because the modeling and awarding of fur coats was involved. This was an outstanding position to take. He is also a vegetarian and an outspoken animal-rights crusader. He said he receives hundreds of supportive letters each year from animal lovers. He and his wife (who died in 1981) loved animals, and he said she stopped wearing a fur coat long before it became fashionable to do so. Bob Barker shares his home with three dogs and two cats, and most of his animals were strays before becoming family. He said he has a reputation, and the animals seem to come to his door. He has also campaigned for animal protection on movie sets and last year was being sued for ten million dollars for statements he made concerning this cruelty.

Sport Hunting Is Unconscionable

I am not qualified to write on hunting and will not attempt to, other than to say I think that this, too, is horrendous, and to share with you some words by David K. Wills, Vice President of Investigations for the Humane Society of the United States. The powerful article on sport hunting that I have before me should be read by every thinking person. It appears in the *HSUS News*, Winter 1991 issue, Vol. 36, No 1. I am sure this magazine could be obtained by writing to this address: HSUS National Headquarters, 2100 L Street, NW, Washington, DC 20037.

This is published quarterly by the HSUS, a non-profit charitable organization. I have been receiving it because of donations we have made. If you make a $10.00 membership donation, it would be a wonderful gift for the animals, and you might also request this issue. In one paragraph, Wills states:

> Now, if any invention was more effectively designed to cause pain than a broadhead arrow (with the possible exception of a steel-jaw trap) I, for one, don't wish to know about it. Imagine a razor-edged projectile penetrating through your skin and flesh, and stopping, lodged deep in the vital organs that keep you alive. The excruciating pain causes you to run blindly, trying to get away from the agony that has engulfed your body. The arrow, which sends a violent reminder of its presence each time you move, is causing you to hemorrhage so that, finally, weakened by bleeding and tortured by a pain that no mind can grasp nor any words describe, you die—a testament to another being's skill with this diabolical weapon.

He concludes this article by saying:

> That any rational person would or could enjoy inflicting pain and causing suffering to another creature is repugnant. Even more offensive is that adult human beings can—and do—rationalize and glorify murder. Both of these observations become more disturbing when we recognize

that this behavior is intentional, and those who engage in sport hunting will put forth every effort to justify their actions. Many will scoff at the suggestion that sport hunting is murder, arguing that murder can be defined as killing a member of our species. It is this type of semantical contortionism that can no longer be allowed to cloak this morally indefensible tradition.

I wish all could read this entire article because it contains so many other facts that all human beings should know about sport hunting. The practice simply cannot be justified, no matter what arguments are used. I have read a number of articles on this subject, but this one has explained all we human beings need to know in regard to it.

Our favorite restaurant, the CooCoo's Nest, here in our little town in New Hampshire, displays a photograph (I do not know how it was taken) on a postcard, taped to the side of the cash register. It is seen by everyone as they pay their checks, and some have suggested the owner get it enlarged. It is a deer in a car, driving with a gun standing visibly in the seat behind him, and a hunter dressed in his bright hunting outfit tied to the hood of the car. Since this picture is in reality seen in reverse during hunting season, it really gives one pause to think. The cartoon has been received most favorably, and I wish I had a copy to include in this book. How horrified some are to see this done to a human, yet many have total disregard for the deer that suffered, died, and got bound to the car.

While reading, I happened to come across the three following quotations. The first is one by Daniel Defoe, quoted in a book called *A Life of One's Own*, by Joanna Field:

> *I saw abundance of fowls, but knew not their kinds, neither, when I killed them, could I tell what was fit for food, and what not. At my coming back, I shot a great bird, which I saw sitting upon a tree, on the side of a large wood. I believe it was the first gun that had been fired there since the creation of the world. I had no sooner fired, but from all the parts of the wood there arose an extraordinary number of fowls, of many sorts, making a confused screaming and crying, every one according to his usual note; but not one of them of any kind that I knew. As for that creature I killed, I took it to be a kind of hawk, its color and beak resembling it, but*

it had no talons or claws more than common: its flesh was carrion and fit for nothing. —Daniel Defoe

This passage upset me so much—the screaming and crying of the fowls because their world had been entered and defiled and one of their members killed. To me the act was so cold-hearted—and the conclusion so harsh and indifferent—that the bird had no value at all. He says, *"fit for nothing."* God did not create that bird to be *"fit for nothing."* A bit of the divine is in all creatures, and it had a purpose—to live and "be," as we all are entitled to do if we are not stricken.

Then, in contrast to the above awful scene, the next evening I was reading some poetry from a lovely old volume. A poem caught my attention, particularly after reading the offensive description (to me) by Daniel Defoe. Please read this poem by William Cullen Bryant now (and more than once, for it grows more beautiful with each reading), and see the amazing contrast between the thoughts and observations of the two authors in seeing and coming upon a fowl. I, for one, choose the writing of W. C. Bryant and feel anew the awe and thrill he felt upon observing this creature of God's.

TO A WATERFOWL
—William Cullen Bryant (1794-1878)
(excerpts, last 5 verses)

There is a Power whose care
Teaches thy way along pathless coast—
The desert and illimitable air—
Lone wandering, but not lost.

All day thy wings have fanned,
At that far height, the cold thin atmosphere,
Yet stoop not weary, to the welcome land,
Though the dark night is near.

And soon that toil shall end;
Soon shalt thou find a summer home, and rest,
And scream among thy fellows; reeds shall bend,
Soon, o'er thy sheltered nest!

> *Thou'rt gone! the abyss of heaven*
> *Hath swallowed up thy form; yet on my heart*
> *Deeply hath sunk the lesson thou hast given,*
> *And shall not soon depart.*

> *He who, from zone to zone,*
> *Guides through the boundless sky thy certain flight,*
> *In the long way I must tread alone*
> *Will lead my steps aright.*

Bryant has touched me deeply through this beautiful poem. He has seen the fowl as a messenger from God to build his own faith, and he respects this amazing creature.

A third passage I wish also to share, for it cannot be forgotten once it is read, and again it depicts man's cruelty. This was found in a book by the wonderful writer Loren Eiseley. The book is *The Night Country*. He has been walking a beach. He writes:

> *A little later in a quieter bend of the shore, I see ahead of me a bleeding, bedraggled blot on the edge of the white surf. As I approach, it starts warily to its feet. We look at each other. It is a wild duck, with a shattered wing. It does not run ahead of me like the longer-limbed gull. Before I can cut off its retreat, it waddles painfully from its brief refuge into the water.*
>
> *The sea continues to fall heavily. The duck dives awkwardly, but with long knowledge and instinctive skill, under the fall of the first two inshore waves. I see its head working seaward. A long green roller, far taller—taller than my head, rises and crashes forward. The black head of the water-logged duck disappears. This is the way wild things die, without question, without knowledge of mercy in the universe, knowing only themselves and their own pathway to the end. I wonder, walking further up the beach, if the man who shot that bird will die as well.*

As I sit here at my desk with window overlooking the lake at night, I hear through the open window the incredibly beautiful sounds of the nightsong of all the birds and creatures of the woods and hear the amazing cry of the loons that leaves one in awe of all that is transpiring in nature at this moment. To see the many varieties of birds coming to the feeders by day and to see the loons diving into the lake out in front of our cottage, or to see the big herons or osprey flying about, just leaves one in wonder. And all of this only cements anew in our hearts that it is an outrage that such creatures as these should be deliberately harmed and killed by humans—as well as any other animals in the world, such as the marvelous dolphins and whales that are suffering and have died horrible deaths.

Vivisection Is an Atrocity

There is only one other subject that I should like to mention before closing this chapter concerning the atrocities that take the lives of animals—and that is vivisection. Much can be read on this in books I have mentioned herein. I will share only one quotation, and perhaps that will be enough to strike your heart. I can barely copy it down, for it has taken me months to come back to it and now be forced to write it so that others may see this hideous practice. It has stayed with me since first I opened *The Extended Circle*, for it is the second quotation in this fine book that I could not be without. The incident related now has been performed without any anesthetic:

> A person who was well-skilled in dissection opened a bitch, and as she lay in most exquisite torture offered her one of her young puppies, which she immediately fell a-licking; and for the time seemed insensible to her own pain; on the removal she kept her eye fixed on it and began a wailing sort of cry which seemed to proceed rather from the loss of her young one that the sense of her own torment. —Joseph Addison

This gentleman has also stated:

> True benevolence, or compassion, extends itself through the whole of existence and sympathizes with the distress of every creature capable of sensation.

I would like to include also a quotation by Tom Regan, who is a member of the Philosophy Department at North Carolina State University. He has written a number of philosophical studies, including the

Case for Animal Rights and *The Expanding Circle*. He is quoted exten-sively on eight-and-a-half full pages in *The Extended Circle*, but I did not obtain the following quotation from those books. In fact, I do not know its source, for my daughter Janna was writing a paper on Animal Rights for one of her courses at West Chester University when I first began to write this book, and she called me to discuss the paper and also to give me several quotations that struck her as very fine. This is the one on laboratory animals:

> *In the case of knowledge of the anatomy and physiology of mamma-lian animals studied in lab sections in high school and university biology, zoology and related courses, this knowledge (of anatomy and physiology) is obtainable without relying on the hands-on experience. Students do not need to dissect any known animals to learn facts about their anatomy and physiology. Detailed drawings of animal anatomy and physiology exist in abundance and are usually included in the very texts used in such courses. On the rights view, to continue to include standard lab sections involving dissection of live mammalian animals is as unnecessary as it is unjustified.*

Vivisection is despicable! If I were to share in a more thorough way, you would be horrified. Please read up on this subject and become informed!

To cut an animal that has not been anesthetized and to proceed to torture this creature in this way—a creature who experiences all the pain and torment we as humans would experience—is an act that cannot be justified in any way, and only the inhumane can exclaim otherwise. If that had been myself, there as described in that quota-tion—pregnant—and I was dissected while feeling fully aware and conscious, and my child removed from me, and then further dissection continued on my body, what then would human beings say concerning my plight! Yet dogs and cats and other animals are held down and tortured in this vile way in the name of science. What will Christians do about this? Is it not a pro-life issue, just as abortion is one? Please, read these books I have told you about—*Animal Liberation, The Extended Circle,* and the others—and write for information also to your nearest Anti-Vivisection League and become informed. To say you do not understand is an excuse for not becoming involved in helping these defenseless animals. I repeat again the quotation by Robert Browning that you will also find in Appendix C:

> *I despise and abhor the pleas on behalf of that infamous practice, vivisection. . . . I would rather submit to the worst of deaths, so far as pain goes, than have a single dog or cat tortured on the pretense of sparing me a twinge or two.*

And Gandhi also has stated:

> *Vivisection is the blackest of all the black crimes that man is at present committing against God and His fair creation.*

And Cardinal Manning (1808-1892) said:

> *Vivisection is a detestable practice. . . . I cannot understand any civilized man committing or countenancing the continuance of such a practice.*

May these writings deeply touch each soul who reads them, and may they lead to each one searching his heart to find what God is saying to him. May you find it in your heart to help and to pray for all God's creatures.

Rochester

CHAPTER NINETEEN

✤

Closing Meditation

"There is not an animal on the earth, not a flying creature on two wings,
but they are people like unto you."
—The Koran

"Be not forgetful to entertain strangers; for thereby some have entertained
angels unawares. Remember them that are in bonds, as bound with them;
and them which suffer adversity, as being yourselves also in body."
—Hebrews 13:2,3 (K.J.V.)

"The greatness of a nation and its moral progress
can be judged by the way its animals are treated."
—M. Gandhi

"I'm holding this cat in my arms so it can sleep, and what more is there."
—Hugh Prather

THE STILL SMALL VOICE

Within my heart I often grieve—
For there are many who believe,
That all God's creatures who are dumb—
To pain and cruelty—must be numb!

They do not know that in the glance
Of speechless animal—there by chance—

If time is taken—soul of the wise
Can understand and recognize—
A discourse splendid and from God—
In silent eyes of those who trod
And share this earth with human creatures—
And that dear dumb ones are His teachers.

If these words that are here penned
One simply cannot comprehend—
Then condescend to please befriend—
And to His Creatures love extend.
Two souls will then know still discourse—
From animal to human—with God as source.

Dedicated to all God's Creatures
Janice Gray Kolb

"The Star Thrower," a true account written by the well-known writer, poet, and anthropologist, Loren Eiseley, forever comes back to haunt my mind and heart since first I read it, and the same must be so concerning others, for the story has been quoted and rewritten in other books and spiritual magazines. It was originally told in so moving a way, and I would like to share it now, for it is worthy to read many times.

At dawn on a beach in Costabel there was a man walking. The beaches there, claims the writer, are littered with the debris of life that the sea rejects. Though they try, they cannot fight their way home through this surf. Repeatedly they are cast back upon the shore. The starfish are among those that are washed up, and their tiny breathing pores are stuffed with sand. To an observer, it would seem that the night sky had showered them down, with the long-limbed starfish were everywhere along the beaches, as far as the eye could see. As the writer, walking along this beach, rounded the next point, he spotted a human figure in the distance, who seemed to him to have the posture of a god. It was a young man, and the writer noticed the young man was picking up starfish, one by one, and flinging them into the sea. When he finally caught up to the youth and stood by his side, he questioned him as to why he was doing this. He answered that if they were left in the morning sun, the stranded starfish would die. The writer, incredulous, exclaimed,

"But there are millions of starfish on this beach. How can you possibly do any good here or make even a small dent in the number of starfish on the shore?" The young man just picked up another starfish, flung it high and far out to sea before continuing on, and said, "There is one that made it!"

This young man was performing a daily task of love by rescuing as many as he could. Perhaps there are those who would think him ridiculous to believe his effort could make a difference, but to each starfish in the young boy's hand that he flung to safety in the waves, it truly did make a difference.

On our journey through life there will be many *starfish* on our paths, and how we meet them and treat them and respond can make a deep difference in our spiritual growth.

A Spectrum of Non-caring

There are those in this world—many Christians included—who do not do harm to animals and creatures, but neither do they show concern for them in any way. It is as if animals should be on another planet—for this one surely belongs only to humans. Total indifference is shown to them, and often thoughtless or disparaging remarks made, if anyone says or does anything in regard to animals to the contrary of this group of indifferent humans' thinking.

Many would not go out of their way to help a creature, and perhaps they would even turn away so as not to become involved, were they to see a situation in which their involvement could make a definite difference.

Many think it is somewhat proper to say they dislike animals—or even that they hate them. Yes, even Christians do this.

And then there are those who would harm animals psychologically. If they would just pause and pray and consider what they are doing, perhaps they would not do it. It is very likely they would not ever do the same thing to a human being. Some are just incredibly thoughtless or ignorant in their knowledge of animals, and others behave this way toward them deliberately. Maybe it is continuously, or just an isolated case, but harm is done to one or more of these innocents.

There are those who are so cruel as to slaughter or kill an animal without thinking there is anything wrong with their actions. There are many ways to kill a creature, and there are many humans who do it in so many various ways. There are humans who get pleasure from this and others who feel they are doing their duty. Christians are included in both these categories. And yet it takes a certain "something" to kill anything, whether as duty, for sadistic pleasure, or for the game of it.

Recently, in thinking and praying about all of this and quietly and deeply reflecting on it all, there seemed to be something unusual come to mind and break through into these sad moments—for any time I think of harm coming to animals in any form, it causes deep sadness to me. I do not know if it was the Holy Spirit speaking to me or just an insight that surfaced from the depths of my being, but it came to me forcibly that perhaps we who hope and long to one day be accepted into Heaven and be given eternal life and welcomed into *"this place"* we await, may find an alarming surprise there.

Heavenly Princes in Disguise

Most of our lives we have been aware of fairy tales and beautifully-created Disney movies made from such stories—of creatures or animals coming into contact with humans. If only a chosen human will give help in some specific way, the specific creature will be set free from a wicked spell and be turned back into his original form of handsome human. Two well-known tales of this sort are "The Frog Prince" and "Beauty and the Beast." There are others, too, that are not as well-known as these. The magic of love, given to the creatures in predesignated ways, brings a transformation, and behold, there stands a human, no longer a frog or a beast!

The insight I had was just this: what if all the creatures God puts into our care here on earth are truly His charmed ones—His princes—His royalty set upon earth to see if we humans are capable of giving them true love, love so endearing that our spirits will mingle with theirs (which they do), thereby transforming them. Then, when we arrive in Heaven, we will recognize in spirit our precious animal companions, who will now be just as we—equal—not beneath us, as many humans thought.

What if these precious animals, which are being slaughtered, hunted, abandoned, experimented upon, and subjected to every known horror including vivisection, will one day no longer be frogs and beasts or cats and dogs and lambs and cows to abuse, but will have dropped these outer garments and be creatures of light and beauty—belonging to Him? They will be shown to us then as having been the glorious means for us, when they were on earth, to advance in spiritual holiness and in the life of self-giving and deep Christian love. And what if we fail? What if those ones we show indifference to or despise or treat in horrendous ways are really divine beings in disguise, but we do not want *"to do unto the least of these."* What if this be so? Please think upon this seriously!

Anyone who has ever had a deep relationship with an animal or has one now, has frequently experienced times when something exists between animal and human that defies explanation—from a dimension not known. And that experience may be often repeated but never less awesome. There comes the distinct feeling, an impression on one's soul, that a being or entity lives within the creature that seems human or divine. I personally have known this repeatedly with my Rochester. It continues to happen as we share our lives. There were moments I specifically remember with one little dog of mine, Lizzie, and most certainly with Katie.

Smile or laugh if you will—but those who have experienced this will not. They will understand what I am saying. Therefore, if there be even the slightest chance that these impressions I have been given in prayer and quietness and solitude even border on the possible—can we risk doing anything to our animal friends that we would not want done to ourselves? Or can we risk indifference and not actively do something to ease their situations and make efforts to protect them and stop the killing?

Are we ready, truly ready, to meet our Lord—or do we have some serious rethinking and prayer to do? Can we allow our senses and souls to be dulled?

Are we ready to meet not only our Lord but the animals, too, that have passed into contact with us in small or large ways—or even the ones that did not, that we never gave a thought or prayed for in their plights, as if they did not exist or were not suffering? Are we in need of confession and forgiveness? Of repentance?

Perhaps, in our pondering, we will be overwhelmingly grateful to still be on earth and have a second chance in regard to the way we view and take a stand for the animals and birds and fish of creation. Perhaps we will know, deep in our spirits, that the God who breathed the breath of life into us, breathed that same breath into His creatures, and we are ALL God's creatures. One group should never cause the other group pain and suffering and death.

Please pray and think on these things, and forevermore be released from *The Ostrich Syndrome*. It is written, *"Thou shalt not kill,"* which includes not only physical killing but also the cruelty of emotional and psychological "slayings."

If we can repeat the Golden Rule (Matthew 7:12) from scripture: *"Do unto others as we would have them do unto us,"* (and every religion has its equivalent of the Golden Rule in its teachings)—and know that we truly follow this in regard to our animals and creatures, as well as to humans—then Our Lord surely must be pleased. But if we cannot—are we truly ready to meet our Maker?

Katrina (Clancy)

Spuds (Clancy)

Afterword

ONCE I HAD COMPLETED THE PREVIOUS CHAPTER, which I had been given in prayer and termed a *meditation,* and had it captured on paper, I knew that I had completed something that was to be told and shared with others. This was not only an inner knowing; I was shown in a very startling and dramatic way by an outward manifestation that the evil one did not want that chapter written and used. At first this manifestation was subtle, and I did not realize what it was. When I did— I knew with all my heart how much God loves the animals and all creatures of His! Let me relate to you what happened, and I have prayed very much for protection before proceeding to write this down now.

I wrote the last chapter in bed in the middle of the night when all was quiet—and as I wrote I began to itch. It began at first on my stomach and tops of my legs, but I was so intent on what I was writing that it was barely annoying. But the more I wrote, the more I itched. When I finished, I slept, and to my knowledge the itching did not continue while my writing ceased. In the morning, I noticed that I had a faint rash on the areas mentioned. Thinking it might be a different detergent we were using, I put other clothing on that had not been washed in it. However, I learned there was no different detergent, upon checking in the basement.

167

Over breakfast at our favorite restaurant, the Coo-Coo's Nest, I enthusiastically told Bob about my writing and completing the final chapter the night before, and we had a deep discussion over it. All the while I itched, trying to be as discreet about it as possible. Once home, we sat down while I read aloud this last chapter to Bob; he affirmed it and was rather in awe at what was written and presented. All the while the itching continued, but I had no time to give to it in my enthusiasm to write.

All afternoon upstairs at my desk overlooking the woods and lake I worked on the last chapter, adding to it the portion about "The Star Thrower." I then transferred all I had written the previous night to the looseleaf paper I use for my manuscript. I had originally written it all on small tablet paper while in bed. As I wrote, the itching began anew and grew worse—and soon most all of me was itching with intensity, and I was scratching frantically my neck, stomach, thighs, arms, chest, and wrists. My lower arms and legs were not in the same condition—nor my back. I was going crazy, but kept writing for several hours at my desk. When I came downstairs and saw areas of my body in the mirror, I was astounded. I had flaming red skin, with huge, raised, defined welts. I decided to take a bath using a different soap, and then I put Vitamin E lotion all over my body. This relieved the itch for some time.

As Bob and I began anew to discuss this chapter—and this itching—we could not at that point understand what was happening. But suddenly the Holy Spirit gave insight, and I realized something I should have realized earlier, due to past experiences. I was experiencing spiritual warfare, because of what I had written about the animals! The phenomenon grew worse after the realization, and before it was time for bed, it was so intense that I grew fearful also. The fear became worse than the itch, and this kind of fear is not of God. My whole back broke out in a hot rash and large welts, and I could not reach it to scratch, which was my deepest intent at the time. Only the Vitamin E lotion relieved it for a period.

Bob gave me some medication that he felt might relieve the symptoms, and I sat in bed and asked him to pray with me three different times. I was unreasonably afraid. As I sat there, I knew I was going to faint, and I became nauseated and ran to the bathroom and lay on the cool floor. I was so sick—but lying on the floor helped me, and I never passed out. Gradually the illness subsided and I made my way back to bed. Bob prayed again, and with my beautiful music playing, as always, the cassette tape of "The Fairy Ring," and Rochester curled on my lap close to me—I was content. Rochester always knows when I am sick or upset and need him. He never leaves—and he stayed there all night. Gradually I began to feel calmer and at peace, and the itching grew less, though welts and rash were all over me. The music played and *"in the Ring"* I grew peaceful, and in the dark drifted to sleep sitting up. In the morning, all red rashes were gone and all welts, except some around my waist. Everywhere else that had been fiery red was now normal. I knew the prayers Bob prayed on my behalf had come against the evil one and we had won the battle. I had never in my life had hives, welts, or rashes, and it was frightening! Yet though I had also been caused to have great fear—it was rewarding to realize and know that what I had written in the Closing Meditation had deep significance. It was significant enough to be worthy of an attack on me for writing it—and then for sharing it with Bob—and transferring it to other manuscript paper. The evil one was truly disturbed and used this attack to attempt to make me back down. But my words have remained as they were first written in the final chapter (the Closing Meditation).

In discussing this later in Pennsylvania with my friend Ginny, who is an ordained Presbyterian pastor as well as a lover and protector of animals, though she did not know the content of my chapter, she stated that she hoped I intended to relate all that happened. Others could see the importance of the insights that had been given and written in the Closing Meditation. This confirmed to me that I should do this, for it had been in my heart to do so.

One night several weeks later when we were again in New Hampshire, I decided to put the account of the spiritual warfare on paper. I had had a very full and productive day writing on this book, and it had been a rewarding and happy time. After a period of relaxing with Bob, I decided to write the account while in bed. As I came through our small kitchen to go into our bedroom just past the kitchen, I picked up a pile of looseleaf paper and my pencil from the table. It was as if I had flipped a switch and at the same time turned off my breathing. It was that instantaneous!! I knew I was in trouble, and I could barely get ready for bed. By the time I had actually accomplished it and gotten in the bed, I was exhausted. Bob had fallen asleep and Rochester again was with me through this difficult time. I sat straight up—hands pressing into mattress, trying to make each breath come up and roll over, and then I would begin again. Readers with asthma will truly understand what I am explaining. I wanted to read or write in my journal, to take my mind from it all, but I could not concentrate except on achieving my next breath. As I struggled for each one, I also struggled to keep calm. Nausea came also. I had come to bed earlier than usual, and the big digital clock opposite me said 11:45 p.m. At 2:45 a.m. I was still wide awake and working at breathing. This is a rather normal hour for me to be awake, writing and praying, but not to be sitting in the same position all those hours, accomplishing nothing but my next breath. By 3:30 a.m. I turned out the light but remained fully awake with Rochester on my lap. Soon the lighted digital clock said 4:30 a.m. I had not slept at all. Rochester and "The Fairy Ring" were my comfort, and the sleeping presence of Bob. Just trying to flip the cassette tape over took so much energy and breath, making me lose ground in my breathing after doing so. But the music was healing and calming, as always, and brought tears on occasion, as it often does. As I sat there at 5:00 a.m., I realized that I had again experienced spiritual warfare, because I had planned to write down the previous account of my experience and the attack of hives (if that is what they were), and had also discussed with Bob that I planned to write it. The mere picking up of the paper and pencil brought the evil one to bear down. I had prayed for myself, not wanting to wake Bob, but I was so weakened that I could not come against him properly. I should have wakened Bob, which is what he said also in the morning when I related all that transpired. Somewhere about 5:30 a.m. I must have fallen asleep. It was the last time I saw the clock. Bob woke me at 8:00 a.m., and with the light had also come a release from the attack. I knew without a doubt that it had been spiritual warfare, and Bob agreed. I knew also that my Closing Meditation must be most significant, that I should have been attacked physically by the evil one, twice! I knew too from the past experience of attack, when I spiritually committed to vegetarianism for the sake of the animals, that the fear that fell upon me and filled me was not of God. It was chilling and evil and unreasonable—out of nowhere to overcome me. I have given this Afterword the title that it has, because the very attacks and opposition I have experienced are hints and indications of affirmation of what I have written in that final chapter about God's creatures.

It is no light thing to have the evil one come against you. The only consolation is knowing there had to be a mighty reason for him to attack.

I can only say once more as I close—that we must all pray and think upon our relationship with His creatures. Perhaps reread the Closing Meditation, for you know now the uproar the writing of it caused. Pray daily and ask God to speak to your soul concerning your personal path, which will lead you closer to His creatures in love and concern and protection.

Learn to look at His creatures in a new way. Pause for individual contact when opportunities present themselves. If you have a fear or dislike of animals, it is not of God, any more than the fear I experienced. God wants us to live in harmony together, and our fellow creatures can bring such love and happiness to human beings. Animals are engaged in many ministries now, and they bring people closer to God. Pray about your fear and ask God to remove it, or ask a spiritual friend to pray with you and build up confidence against that fear. God will take it away, but you must take that first willing step and *want it* removed. Do not settle for less and thereby forever estrange yourself from the fullness and harmony of life on this earth that God desires for all His creatures.

Ask to be shown in prayer what you can do to make His earth a safe and humane place for His animals to exist. Pray for their welfare, and in doing this I believe He will reveal to you your own special way for changing things in this world to help stop horrendous acts against animals, so that they, too, can live out their individual lives, just as you hope to continue to live out yours. To excuse yourself from even trying is the same as allowing them to be tortured and slain. You may not do the actual despicable acts and killings—but neither are you doing one thing to stop them! It is one and the same. Apathy and indifference are killers, just as much as the slaughterers. Albert Schweitzer has said, *"The quiet conscience is an invention of the devil."* Whose ambassadors are we in this world? God's or the devil's? Remember, *the same Breath that Breathed life into you Breathed it also into His creatures.* That fact alone should confront each soul in a collision impact and never again permit anyone to disregard another life, be it human or of another species. To say you would never harm an animal, yet allow atrocities to continue against them, is not of God. No being likes to suffer. Therefore, do not inflict suffering either directly or through your own fears and apathy. *"Do unto others as you would have them do unto you,"* and remember the way of Ahimsa—that of non-violence. Pray much and remember that *"non-human creatures are not merely objects to be used for our pleasure or instruments for human purposes, but are of value in themselves and to God."* (World Council of Churches)

If we can just become gentle and child-like and think each day upon the following simple well-known prayer-poem, perhaps His light will illumine more brightly our souls and we will never again take the life of a creature of God's for granted. We will listen and be led by that still small voice and learn what each one of us can do personally to save the animals, birds, fish, whales, dolphins, and all things that have breath. May we prayerfully repeat now that simple poem?

> *Dear Father, hear and bless*
> *Thy beasts and singing birds,*
> *And guard with tenderness*
> *Small things that have no words.*
> —Anonymous

O Heavenly Father,
protect and bless all things
that have breath;
guard them from all evil
and let them sleep
in peace. . . .
Amen and Amen.
—Albert Schweitzer

In loving memory of
Misty (Clancy)

APPENDIX A

Poems for Meditation: In Reverence of All God's Creatures

"I think I could turn and live with animals, they're so placid and self-contained: I stand and look at them long and long."
—Walt Whitman

FOR MANY YEARS I have been collecting poems that I love. I have written them in journals so that I would not have to search for any of these in individual books if I wanted again to read and enjoy them. Many of these poems were poems about animals and all of God's Creatures. Several I have loved since I was a child. I have continued this collection into the present and you will find an assortment of them in this chapter.

Along with those poems of more well-known poets are original poems by a number of poet friends of mine, family members, one by my husband, and a selection of my own poems. All of this poetry is included here to show you the beauty of God's Creatures and their profoundness. Many depict merely why they are on earth and reveal how they do just what God intended them to do. A number of poems show the depth of exchange that can be experienced between human and creature—

sometimes in the mere glance or holding with the eyes—or in some cases much more. Look for those lines that speak of such discourse. Often they are subtle or briefly stated yet are the basis and reason for the poem.

Other poems speak of cruelty to God's Creatures and reactions to this that strike the heart's core, especially if perpetrated by the writer.

All of these poems are life-affirming and try to show the reader that we must truly pray and think upon our relationship with the animals, birds, insects, and fish of this world. When you read these poems and go back to them again and again to meditate on them, I feel you will experience God's touch on your soul and a new, more spiritual way to view His Creatures. —J.G.K.

THE NOBLE OSTRICH

The ostrich is a noble bird
With rumors 'bout him quite absurd.
They say when things don't go as planned
He puts his head into the sand.

The truth of this if it be told
Is that the ostrich is quite bold.
When listening for a distant sound
His ear is placed down on the ground.

He then looks up and knows the scope
Of things with which he'll have to cope.
But from a distance it appears
His head is covered—not just ears.

But folklore has distorted facts
And says that fear has caused these acts.
And when unpleasant things evolve
Escape is sure—the problem solved.

We humans are a lot like this.
We value happiness and bliss—

And try to keep our armor strong
So we won't have to deal with wrong.

We see the evil things around
And promptly put our heads in ground.
And go along our merry way
With thoughts of joy and fun and play.

So when from facts we want to hide
The truth's ignored—we're occupied—
With other things that comfort us
Tidy things that cause no fuss.

The issue here is animal rights.
We take hard looks and view the plights—
Of these poor creatures who cannot speak
But we are strong and they are weak.

So we must now not hide in sand.
Instead we've got to lend a hand—
And face the real and often cruel
To help these creatures who we rule.

Don't be a person who can't see
Or one who shows such apathy.
For those who can't defend their rights
Lets state their case and fight their fights.

The "Ostrich Syndrome" is the name
For this sad circumstance of shame
For those of us who hide and say
I just don't think of them that way.

So consider "lower life" my friend,
Compassion for these lives we tend.
Stop hiding with your buried eyes
And never see the pain and lies.

—Robert A. Kolb Jr.

On Cruelty to Animals

He is no Christian in his deeds
Who slays in wantonness of power
The weakest life whose tiny needs
    Betray it in a fatal hour.
Who blots from time the humblest share
Of that abundant life which throngs
The free domains of earth and air,
But has no voice to plead its wrongs.

Oh, ye who scornfully regard
A helpless creature's dumb appeal,
Were not your fate unjustly hard,
If that great power to whom ye kneel
Should spurn your sorrow when ye pray,
And thrust you from the world, to be
A jest for fiends—to drift away,
A wreck upon Oblivion's sea?

Has God created life for naught,
That ye should trample under foot
The seal of his creative thought,
Stamped on the lowliest, feeblest brute?
When ye remember what ye are,
How low in thee Immortal eyes,
No creature on this sinful star
Seems meet for mortals to despise
No! by that mercy which delays
To judge your folly or your vice—
By that one star whose gracious rays
Still point you back to Paradise—
Be merciful; stoop not to break
The cup of life, however frail,
Lest every ruin that you make
Should cause in you some good to fail.

—George Castle Rankin
(died March 22, 1882—21 years old)

HEALER

Often when I am sad,
concerned or ill—
He'll clasp both paws around my hands
with a will
To make me right.
And soon will come light.

He'll never leave my lap—
nor ever nap.
Long hours shall pass
he'll hold me fast—
For he is there to heal—
and it is precious and surreal.

He is God's Angel, in disguise—
a joy forever—my divine surprise.

—J.G.K.

🐾

Four ducks on a pond,
A grass-bank beyond,
A blue sky of spring,
White clouds on the wing:
What a little thing
To remember for years—
To remember with tears!

—William Allingham

He prayeth best who loveth best
All things both great and small;
For the dear God who loveth us,
He made and loveth all.

—Samuel Taylor Coleridge (1772-1834)
(from the "Rime of the Ancient Mariner")

ANGEL BEING

With all my soul I know that he—
Was sent from heaven just for me.
An angel in soft marmalade fur,
Large golden eyes—deep soothing purr.
He speaks to me without a word—
And yet each message I have heard.

The silence shared throughout the days—
Ministering in mysterious ways—
Ever with me—his small being—
Confirms it is Angel I am seeing!

Beneath my heart he sleeps each night—
And keeps it whole—warm with his light.
There is no need to see his wings—
Just seeing him—and my soul sings!

—J.G.K., *written for Rochester*

WHERE IS IT?

He flips his tail
And points his nose
And digs it up

With frantic claws—
That nut he buried
Long ago
When there wasn't
Any snow.
He holds it tight
Between his paws
Cracks it with
His little jaws
And eats it up,
Then off he goes . . .

But how is he sure a nut's still there?
And how can he guess exactly where?
Squirrel never needs to guess
He knows.

—Unknown

ON THE GRASSHOPPER AND THE CRICKET

The poetry of earth is never dead:
When all the birds are faint with the hot sun
And hide in cooling trees, a voice will run
From hedge to hedge about the new-mown mead-
That is the Grasshopper's. He takes the lead
In summer luxury; he has never done
With his delights, for when tired out with fun
He rests at ease beneath some pleasant weed.
The poetry of earth is ceasing never:
On a lone winter evening when the frost
Has wrought a silence, from the stove there shrills
The Cricket's song, in warmth increasing ever,
And seems to one in drowsiness half lost,
The Grasshopper's among some grassy hills.

—John Keats

ANGEL NOTES

This morning as I sat in prayer
A tinkling fell upon the air
Just in the hall outside my door.
Then in the room there came still more
Delicate music to my right
And yet there was no one in sight.

Rochester here upon my lap,
Instantly rose up from his nap
To listen then along with me—
Faced to his right—and seemed to see.
And when the music stilled—we two—
Stared in each other's eyes—we knew!

—J.G.K.

🐾

ROMY'S THANK YOU NOTE

Thank you for your prayer so true
Now I'm feeling all brand new.
It's not much fun being sick.
I could not play or do a trick.
But now I'm feeling very fine.
Look at my coat, it really shines!
I once was puffy, full of air;
Thanks again for your prayer!

—Don Richards
To Jan from Don (for Romy)
(from Don's loving and handsome cat
following recovery after an illness)

PLEASE HONK FOR SERVICE

A little black duck today came to call
He walked up the beach and o'er the rock wall.
He waddled around—made a honk now and then—
Announcing arrival and also his yen—
For pieces of bread that he knows are in store,
(For his family has visited this cottage before.)

The nice man obliged and threw him the treat—
(The duck has no preference—either white or whole wheat.)
We watched him devour each piece on the ground
That fell to surround him—then turning around—
He gazed at us steadfastly with dark little eyes—
Walked back down the beach with honks of goodbyes

—Janice Gray Kolb
Dedicated to Balch Lake Ducks

FAILED RESCUE

This evening as I take a bath—
Around the tub on self made path—
An insect strides the slippery side—
And I vaguely take some pride,
That his footing is so sure—
He has the spunk to so endure.

My thoughts then turn to other things—
Then he is gone—took off on wings.
At least that's then what I assume—
I do not know he's met his doom!
But as I step from tub to floor—
I see that little bug once more!

My heart then sinks—for there he floats—
And I am sure if taking votes—

'Twould not be rescues for that mite—
Who slipped in water late tonight.

But I grab the soap dish there—
And in hurry and despair,
I dip that little body out—
Just in case there is a doubt.

I let him stay in dish to dry—
Inside I say, "O please don't die!"
And yet I know that little dear—
Cannot move—will still be here—
In the morning when I wake
And I feel sadness for his sake.

Somehow I cannot comprehend
I did not save him in the end.
Life's insecure—I did not see
That bug slip in the tub with me.

—Janice Gray Kolb
Dedicated to the little bug

I WOULD NOT ENTER ON MY LIST OF FRIENDS

I would not enter on my list of friends
(Though graced with polished manners and fine sense,
Yet wanting sensibility) the man
Who needlessly sets foot upon a worm.
An inadvertent step may crush the snail
That crawls at evening in the public path;
But he that has humanity, forewarned,
Wilt tread aside and let the reptile live.

—William Cowper

A Robin Red Breast in a cage
Puts all Heaven in a rage . . .
A Skylark wounded in the wing
A Cherubim does cease to sing.

—William Blake

NORA

Only once did I have the joy of meeting
Nora. Her quiet being and soulful greeting
As I came up the walk
caused me to pause and talk
With this velvet, gray creature who sat in the grass
staring at me with soft, green eyes. I could not pass
Without conversation
and loving admiration
For Rose-Beth's sweet companion and treasure.

O, I am grateful to have had this pleasure—
for had I not paused to note Nora's beauty and
incomparable worth—
I would have missed a glory now passed from earth.

—J.G.K.

TO A DOG

If there is no God for thee,
Then there is no God for me.

—Anna Hempstead Branch

GOD'S BEACH CREATURES

God's little creatures are all around.
You look to your left, right or just up and down.
There's a crab, a turtle, a seagull or a gnat.
They all have a purpose so let's treat them like that.

—Jessica Mae Kolb Drakely

HONESTY

I never heard a sparrow cry
in pity for the rain,
or a squirrel or a mouse apologize
for scarin' me to death.

I never heard a cow complain
bout summer's sunburned days
Or never heard a frog repent
and swear to mend his ways.

I never knew a cat who prayed
or a dog who went to church.
Or a pigeon
or a pig
or a horse or a chicken
who practiced daily prayer.

But I know these special souls
have dignity and worth
and an admirable honesty
that enriches life on earth.

—Francis Egan

SILENT FLIGHT

Over the waters the large bird soared—
And landing in our cove—could not be ignored.
His very majestic presence—and stance
(By mere chance we had observed)—seemed to enhance
The scene. Could this great blue heron in his pause
Sense our appreciation and souls' applause?
In the silences of two humans and a bird—
Only the gentle uniting wind of the Spirit could be heard.

—J.G.K.

🐾

THE CRICKET

Little inmate, full of mirth
Chirping on my kitchen hearth
Wheresoe'er be thine abode
Always harbinger of good
Pay me for thy warm retreat
With a song more soft and sweet;
In return thou shalt receive
Such a strain as I can give.

Neither night nor dawn of day
Puts a period to thy play:
Sing then—and extend thy span
Far beyond the date of man:
Wretched man, whose years are spent
In repining discontent
Lives not, aged though he be,
Half a span, compared with thee.

—William Cowper

NIGHTSONG

This night God called a sweet convention
Upon my ear this intervention
Lifts my soul to new dimension
Far beyond my comprehension.

To my hidden observatory
Come strains from a conservatory
That fill the night and so resound
Throughout deep woods that here surround.

Celestial choir of migratories
Bring to earth their heavenly glories—
Chords so utterly spiritualistic
Incomprehensible—haunting—mystic.

Birdsong—O such lilting sound—
And little creatures so profound
Join the choirs of God's creation
Giving my heart jubilation.

Insects, beasties—birds of feather
Blend sweet harmony together
All tiny voices sing in fervor—
Nightsong gift to this observer.

—Janice Gray Kolb

My little dog:
A heart-beat at my feet.

—Edith Wharton

THE CLEANING CREW

Little figures small and brown
Are here to clean up what falls down—
From the feeders overhead
The seeds for birds and crumbs of bread.

Their little mouths are open wide.
Their tummies fat and full inside.
Dear little chipmunks—such a stir!
Vacuum cleaners made of fur!

—Janice Gray Kolb

ANGELIC HOST

He sits upon my lap—gazing into my eyes—
All love—and fully aware I know his disguise
Revealed to me compassionately through the years—
In tender moments—or when I've needed breath—or been in tears.
And so when his gaze shifts to beyond my shoulder
And his eyes widen to become rounder and golder
In recognition—and he moves his stare slowly to the ceiling
Then climbs gently up my being in that direction—I should be kneeling!
For I am in the presence of Angels that have to me been shown—
Through his awe and reverence—and made known
By one who is one—and welcomes others here from day to day.
I feel their silent presence come our way.
And in this small room I sit in splendor—dumfounded–
For by Angels I am daily surrounded.

I do not yet have his eyes to see.
I only know a feline Angel lives with me.

—Janice Gray Kolb
dedicated to Rochester—and our Angels

CAT NAP

Now we are in bed—
the day we have shed.
I put down my book
just to look.
Stretched out from head to toe
between my feet—
So apropos
in all the heat—
Is my precious friend—
blessed dividend.

White paw draped across his face—
I want to embrace
His little form—
but the night is too warm.
I let him sleep
to count his sheep.
Caressing his soft fur
I hear his purr.
I kiss the tip of his tail
and slowly inhale
His goodness—and his light—
and with a prayer—gently whisper—
"Good night."

—J.G.K.

VOICE OF THE VOICELESS

O never a brute in the forest and never a snake in the fen
Or ravening bird, starvation stirred, has hunted its prey like men.
For hunger and fear and passion alone drive beasts to slay.
But wonderful man, the crown of the plan, tortures and kills for play.

—Ella Wheeler Wilcox

MIRROR IMAGES

"Pets mirror their masters,"
I've often heard said.
What images ours send
Oft fills me with dread.

Now, Dawn Alice, the dog
Is gentle and sweet.
To be considered like her
Would be a real treat.

Luanne is disdainful,
A haughty, proud, cat.
Does anyone really
See me like that?

Felicity suffered and
Lived in great pain.
Do I suffer in silence?
Has my life been in vain?

The parakeets live peacefully,
Though one's yellow, one's blue.
Do race or color matter
When my fellows I view?

Here in our home
All live in love and in peace.
May this be the reflection
That everyone sees!

—Peggy Dirvin

❧

How strange is human pride!
I tell thee that those living things,
To whom the fragile blade of grass,
That springeth in the morn
And perisheth ere noon,
Is an unbounded world;
I tell thee that those viewless beings,
Whose mansion is the smallest particle
Of the impassive atmosphere,
Think, feel and live like man;
That their affections and antipathies,
Like his, produce the laws
Ruling their moral state;
And the minutest throb
That through their frame diffuses,
The slightest, faintest motion,
Is fixed and indispensable
As the majestic laws
That rule yon rolling orbs.

—Percy Bysshe Shelley ("Queen Mab")

To What Purpose this Waste?

And other eyes than ours
Were made to look on flowers.
Eyes of small birds and insects small:
The deep sun-blushing rose
Round which the prickles close
Opens her bosom to them all.
The tiniest living thing
That soars on feathered wing,
Or crawls among the long grass out of sight
Has just as good a right
To its appointed portion of delight
As any King.

—Christina Rossetti

EPITAPH TO A DOG
*(Lord Byron's tribute to "Boatswain" on a monument
in the garden of Newstead Abbey)*

Near this spot
Are deposited the Remains
Of one
Who possessed Beauty
Without Vanity,
Strength without Insolence,
Courage without Ferocity,
And all the Virtues of Man
Without his Vices.

This Praise, which would be unmeaning flattery
If inscribed over Human Ashes,
Is but a just tribute to the Memory of
"Boatswain," a Dog
Who was born at Newfoundland,
May 1803,
And died at Newstead Abbey
November 18, 1808

Ye, who perchance behold this simple urn,
Pass on—it honors none you wish to mourn.
To mark a friend's remains these stones arise;
I never knew but one—and here he lies.

—George Gordon, Lord Byron

🐾

THEIR LIVES ARE IMPORTANT AS ALL HE CREATED

The Heavenly Father up above
Has sent the animals for us to love.

To cherish, caress, to care for with joy
As did our Jesus when he was a boy.

The lesson to learn from our animal friends
Answer life's question on whom to depend.

They do not sow, they do not reap
Yet by Him they are housed and they eat.

Their example of calmness and faith and of trust
Is something the Father desires in us.

Be mindful the time that He has taken
Do not destroy what He has awakened.

Accept these creatures as important to Him
Know if we kill them it too is a sin.

Thank you dear Lord for all you have made
Open my mind to the plan you have laid.

—Jane Michener Kroll

MY FRIEND THE ROBIN

Having upturned many spades of earth
in my private garden space,
I stood soldier straight
To put my sinews back in place.
I looked about, and then toward the fence,
There perched a robin
Making a survey quiet and intense.
To inspect my handiwork he didn't care,
It was for food he hoped I'd share.

I felt a companion touch
As I back-slided and made my exit.
I went in for tea,
And watched through the curtain.
He swooped down, no need for searching:
It was now to get his share.
I kept my watch,
And saw him fly back again.
It was no time for glutting
And no fancy strutting,
With mouths to feed
He made a promise to succeed.

—Samuel Vincent Fasy, Jr.

CONSOLATION

When I have a problem or trial in my life
Or have deadlines I just haven't met
I've yet not to find great comfort
In the eyes of my dear sweet pet.

She offers a constant abiding love
In the face of my problems and pain
It's the kind of love I've found only in prayer
As I push towards Heavenly gain.

When I'm not understood or I can't understand
The odd circumstances of life
I know when I turn to my "Molly" dog
My heart will be eased of its strife.

She is constant and true and depends on my care
To sustain her as life moves along
I can only hope that she's half as blessed
As the one to whom she belongs.

—June Leslie Kolb Hudson

WHO WAKES THE BIRDS?

Who wakes the birds?
Who tells them it's time?
Where is their clock?
Is it hunger
or time to sing,
or stretch the wing?
Because they do what
they're born for,
and infinitely so.

—Samuel Vincent Fasy, Jr.

A BIRD

Father in thy starry tent
I kneel, a humble supplicant.
A bird has died today on earth.
Of little worth,
Yet very dear.
Gather him in Thy arms
If only for awhile.
I fear he will be lonely;
Shield him with Thy smile.

—Source unknown

LIZZIE

A little Irish lass was she
Who came to us from 'cross the sea;
She came into our home to be
Part of our fine family.

Eliza Brehon was her name
And her tiny leg was lame.
Her little furrowed brow showed worry
As 'round our house she'd daily hurry.

For such a young one and so small
She took our burdens one and all.
She seemed to have them in her heart
And carried them right from the start.

From the winter that she came
We were never quite the same.
She was a Mama's girl we knew
Enhancing life—remaining true.

She'd look at us with her dear eyes
Concern was there 'til her demise.
Our little one was such a worrier
A dainty pedigreed Cairn Terrier.

—Janice Gray Kolb
Dedicated to Eliza Brehon Kolb, "Lizzie"
September 7, 1990, Her birthday

🐾

MORNING ENCAMPMENT

Walking one morning, in the early mist
and dew, I came across a miracle,
A brigade of God's Holy Angels.
They were magnificent birds from the north,
taking their rest in a field.
Their sentries gave no alarm,
for they knew I was a friend.
We spent time together in silent communion,
these magnificent geese and I.
The birds were quietly grazing on the grass,
myself learning from these fine birds.
Then, as if on a given signal, the whole
flock took to flight, singing and calling,
the mere sight of it singing praises to the Lord.
I learned a lesson that morning,
that God is supreme, His creation magnificent.
As the birds went their way and I went mine,
I praised the Lord for what I had learned:
That all life is Holy, a gift from God,
that can never be repaid.
Thank you Lord for Your way,
Thank you for Your presence,
Thank you for Your wonder.

—Barry Richard Greene
For God's Wonder

❧

MOUSE HOUSE

In our home there is a House.
It's decorated for a mouse.
Invented by a man of God—
Whose hope it is no one will trod,
Or torture, poison little mice.
That's why this Mouse House is so nice.

It is a Pro-Life trap, you see.
He catches mice and sets them free!
Peanut butter and jelly beans—
Entice each mouse and are the means
To tempt his entrance through the door,
Then it closes—that's the core—
And it's the basis—to enwrap
Each tiny mouse in Mouse House trap.

Then man takes the House outside,
Raises door up very wide.
A wiggling little nose peeks through.
Little eyes then search for clue—
To see if there is anyone—
To block his path when he will run.
If you could see this little face—
Never again could you erase—
Or take a life in apathy.
Thou shalt not kill is God's decree!

—Janice Gray Kolb
Dedicated to Bob, to mice—
and to all non-violence

ENCOUNTER

Driving along Route 110—a dark and wooded place
In West Newfield, Maine—with not an evident trace
Of other life—there suddenly appeared a deer from out the brush—
Caught in our headlights—and about to rush—
Before us across the road.
And we—startled, and about to explode
In excitement—began swerving
To the right—keeping him in sight—and though unnerving—
We would not have missed this moment of seeing
This handsome large antlered buck—or of being
There—at that very time—and in that space—
And to have had the honor of meeting him face to face.

—J.G.K.

DUCK DOCK

Little ducks all in a cluster—
Feathers shining with sun-touched luster—
Are gathered silently in meditation
Obviously deep in contemplation.
Deserted red dock tucked in the cove—
Has become their treasure-trove—
Where dreams are spun—at least begun—
They sun-bathe there in summer sun.

Gazing out upon the lake—
They now partake in quiet break.
For just as humans go apart
In silence and for peace of heart—
So too, dear creatures sun and pray—
Commune with God in their own way.
Ducks are fortified for life's long swims—
In these sweet daily interims.

—Janice Gray Kolb

THE RESTING PLACE

The little baby on the hood
clung for his dear life.
He wasn't to blame when he was maimed
and fell from the limb above.
The little baby on the hood
clutched the shiny metal.
The branches and leaves surrounded him,
and his pillow was a petal.
His mama had left him just moments before
to gather up some dinner—
And in that time a scavenger picked a fight
and became a winner.

The car was parked beneath the tree
where baby's family stayed.
But when the pest attacked the nest,
birdie chirped and prayed.
Several hours came and went—
the little baby slept.
God saw him lying on the hood,
and his soul he kept.

The woman came to drive to work,
but stopped beside her car—
She spied the fragile baby bird
lying—not too far.
She gently scooped the baby from
its temporary home.
And placed him in the fallen nest
where he and Mom
could quietly rest.

—Barbara Jan Kolb Egan

🐾

TO AN ANT

Tonight as I made dinner—
On the counter top I found—
(O dear God was I the sinner?)
An ant so bound and round.

He was wound into a ball
And he could not get undone
And his hair-like legs so small
Tangled so he could not run!

Had this giant that is me
With a pot or glass or dish—
Hurt him so unknowingly?
O dear God 'twas not my wish!

I tried fervently to free him—
With thin paper—gentle touch—
He was crippled—hope was dim,
He could not know how very much—

I prayed, and then with tears—
Made a place for him until—
He'd be found by all his peers,
On my quiet window sill.

O Dear Lord—it is a life!
Forgive me if I caused it strife!
But if I did not harm him—please—
Won't you put my heart at ease?

Is he screaming there in fright?
O help that tiny ant tonight!

—Janice Gray Kolb

❧

AN ANGEL'S TOUCH

We hold hands when we're alone.
This is only known
by one or two—
but I will tell you
That it is the most moving thing,
like the brush of an Angel's wing—
To feel that soft, small white paw—
feather-light with no hint of claw
Resting on my hand.
Only few can understand.

Then I place my other hand upon his paw—
and it is the dearest phenomenon I ever saw—
For he then puts his other paw on me—
(and I do not want to be free!)
And our little stack of love and affection
at times brings tears—and reflection—
Upon our life together and moments captured
for we two so alike—become enraptured
By the simplest things—
as paws brushing hands like Angels' wings

—Janice Gray Kolb
dedicated to Rochester

MY FOUR FRIENDS

Molly's an excitable thing.
She loses all control.
When guests come to visit,
To greet them is her goal.

She wiggles and yips and spins
And places her head in your hand.
But if you say one cross word,
She'll bury her head in the sand.

Kelly is a tiny wonder
A little acrobat is she.
She leaps and bounds and frolics
For all her friends to see.

Although she may be boisterous,
Won't settle down sometime,
She can be a cuddle bunny
And quiet as a mime.

Stuffy is adventurous
And loves to wander free.
Whether rolling in who-knows-what
Or squirrel-chasing up a tree.

She's always looking for excitement,
She's always looking for fun.
But watch out 'cause—AHHH
Here she comes!

Pepper is a gentleman,
He contemplates 'neath trees.
I sometimes think that he forgets
That he's an animal with fleas.

He's been a good buddy
And always lends an ear,
He senses if you're upset
And kisses away each fear.

Molly, Kelly, Stuffy—
And Pepper are four friends of mine
We walk, play, hang out
And get along just fine.

They may not talk, but that just doesn't matter
After all, talk can just be idle chatter.

—Janna R. Kolb VanDorick

To a Fish of the Brooke

Why flyest thou away with fear?
Trust me, there's naught of danger near.
I have no wicked hooke
All covered with a snaring bait,
Alas, to temp thee to thy fate.
And dragge thee from the brooke.

O harmless tenant of the flood,
I do not wish to spill thy blood,
For Nature unto thee
Perchance hath given a tender wife,
And children dear, to charm thy life,
As she hath done for me.

Enjoy thy stream, O harmless fish;
And when an angler for his dish,
Through gluttony's vile sin,
Attempts, a wretch, to pull thee out,
God give thee strength, O gentle trout,
To pull the raskall in!

—J. Wolcot

The Fly

Little fly,
Thy summer's play
My thoughtless hand
Has brush'd away.

—William Blake

PURRING PAPERWEIGHT

What could be more beautiful than this—
Dear cat contemplating in silent bliss.
Upon my desk in unmoving pose.
So pure of heart—free of life's woes.

Profiled in window—backdrop of trees—
Wafting through screen—the gentle breeze—
Entices closing eyes to slowly raise
Upon blue lake in meditating gaze.

He nobly sits—so utterly trusting.
Because I love him—I am adjusting.
For on my papers he has been alighting—
Until he moves—I cease that writing.

I take my pencil and wastepaper scrap—
And pen this poem on my lap.
Sweet honorable companion—eternal friend.
In your faithful presence, I choose to bend.

—Janice Gray Kolb
Dedicated to Rochester

❧

TO A SKYLARK

Hail to thee, blithe Spirit!
Bird thou never wert,
That from heaven or near it,
Pourest thy full heart
In profuse strains of unpremeditated art.

Higher still and higher
From the earth thou springest
Like a cloud of fire;

The blue deep thou wingest,
And singing still dost soar, and soaring ever singest

Like a Poet hidden
In the light of thought
Singing hymns unbidden,
Till the world is wrought
To sympathy with hopes and fears it heeded not:

Teach us, Sprite or Bird,
What sweet thoughts are thine:
I have never heard
Praise of love or wine
That panted forth a flood of rapture so divine.

Teach me half the gladness
That thy brain must know,
Such harmonious madness
From my lips would flow;
The world should listen then—as I am listening now!

—P.B. Shelly

THE LEAST*

Dear little animals too have fear
And sense when danger hovers near.
They cannot put a gas mask on—
Yet anxiously await the dawn.
They need the help of humans true—
'Neath all the fur they're children too!
And all are precious in His sight—
O God save them in this Dark Night.

—Janice Gray Kolb
*Dedicated to all the animals caught in the war of Desert Storm
January 1991*
*Words of Jesus - "If you have done it unto the least of these—you have done it unto Me"

LITTLE PAWS

This is a prayer for little paws
All up and down the land:
Driven away, no friendly voice,
Never an outstsretched hand.

For weary little paws of beasts
Torn and stained with red.
And never a home and never a rest
Till little beasts are dead.

O God of homeless things, look down
And try to ease the way
Of all the little weary paws
That walk the world today.

—Source Unknown

NO TITLE NEEDED

Roses are red, Violets are blue
Help the animals to be safe—
Because God loves them too.
Why don't you feed and pet them—
And love them a lot
And they will lick you—
A lot of times.

—Poem by Julia Rose Hudson, Sketch by Jesse Robert Gottlieb,
Grandchildren of author, both done at age 8.

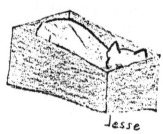

MY ROMEO

My cat, he means a lot to me;
He understands my poetry
And comforts me when I am sad.
Sometimes he even makes me mad!

But I am very much aware
That he depends upon my care.

He meows, he speaks, he almost shouts,
He knows it's time to put food out.
He does remind, he's almost rude,
But only saying, "I NEED FOOD!"

Yes, you could say I love my cat,
We are a pair, and that is that!

—Don Richards

Do you know how hard a bird will work
to make a nest?
She's like a human parent, 'cause she wants
the very best.
One little Robin proved this point
on my front porch last spring.
She sat upon my hanging plant,
and then when she took wing,
I looked into this flowering pot,
a nest was built with care.
So finely woven through the grass
was freshly cut red hair.
Who knew as I cut Tim's soft curls,
she watched from trees above.
Then waited till we left to build,
her home so full of love.

—Laurel Elizabeth Kolb Gottlieb

LANDSCAPES

Out of the windows of my eyes,
I contemplate what nature wants to share
And of these moments am taken
out of earthly ties.
While in my trance and all my thoughts replete
I use the given lenses from above that
make it all complete.
Now with heart and eyes I'm freed to see
the beauty of it all.
With trees so tall,
and meadows soaked with dew.
Birds and bees, and flowers too,
Rocks and rills
surround the hills.
Now a rabbit and a squirrel catch me
In their stare,
With blinking eyes,
they look upward to the skies,
Taking a moment to decide
Graciously do they say:
"Okay, we'll let him share."

—Samuel Vincent Fasy Jr.

BEHOLDEN

How can I ever give adequate thanks—
For a small, beloved creature
Who truly and most certainly ranks
With the Angels—a spiritual teacher
To my soul.
He made me whole—
And allowed me to see beauty
And truth—and instilled a duty
Within my being—
Call it a freeing—

Of overwhelming love and devotion
For all of God's Creatures.
A deep and intense emotion
To be one of the beseechers
Called on their behalf—
To write paragraph after paragraph
For the Animals' Rights—
To make known their plights.
My little cat
Did all of that!
I am enriched—emboldened!
To one with eyes love-filled and most golden—
I am beholden.

—Janice Gray Kolb
Dedicated to my dear little Rochester on his birthday, May 30, 1994

KINSHIP

I am the voice of the voiceless;
Through me the dumb shall speak,
Till the deaf world's ear be made to hear
The wrongs of the wordless weak.

From street, from cage and from kennel,
From stable and zoo, the wail
Of my tortured kin proclaims the sin
Of the mighty against the frail.

Oh, shame on the mothers of mortals
Who have not stooped to teach
Of the sorrow that lies in dear dumb eyes,
The sorrow that has no speech.

The same force formed the sparrow
That fashioned man the king;
The God of the whole gave a spark of soul
To furred and to feathered thing.

And I am my brother's keeper,
And I will fight his fight,
And speak the word for beast and bird,
Till the world shall set things right.

—Ella Wheeler Wilcox

❧

HIGHER GROUND SONG

Large Mourning Doves
and little loves
like Chickadees—
Eat all they need
of seed—and feed
beneath birch trees.

The cooing song
is oh, so strong
upon the air.
Delightful birds
send out their words
on strains so fair.

Such harmony
and melody
beside the lake;
Birds of a feather
sing together
for His sake.

—Janice Gray Kolb

❧

SNOW GAZERS

My friend and I sit side-by-side
Gazing out of the window—we just cannot hide—
Our pleasure and joy at what we behold—
Millions of snowflakes out there in the cold.
He turns and looks at me as if to say,
"I cannot imagine a more wondrous day."
And then we continue to lovingly stare—
(He on my desk and I on the chair.)
His uplifted eyes try to follow each flake
And he guides many down to earth and to lake.

He turns once again to me—blinks in deep love—
Then his eyes seem to draw down more flakes from above.
Framed in our pane is a work of great art—
The Creator has sent it—it brightens the heart.
And while my blessed friend and I sit in the quiet—
Inside our beings is an unutterable riot.

—Janice Gray Kolb
dedicated to Rochester

Rochester

There are, of course, many more inspiring poems that could be included, and I would like to mention a few that I encourage you to find and enjoy.

"The Snare" by James Stephens;
"The Bells of Heaven" and "Stupidity Street" by Ralph Hodgson;
"The Worm" by Thomas Ginsborne;
"Bete Humaine" by Frances Brett Young
in *The Extended Circle: A Commonplace Book of Animal Rights*, compiled by Jon Wynne-Tyson, New York: Paragon House, 1989.

"To My Dog 'Blanco'" by Josiah Gilbert Holland;
"The Cow" by Robert Louis Stevenson
found in *Poems of Creatures Large and Small*, edited by Gail Harvey, New York: Avenel Books, 1991.

"Recovery" by Rabindranath Tagore, in *Selected Poems*, translated by William Radice, New York: Viking Penguin, 1985.

"The Gusts of Winter Are Gone" from *The Greek Poets*;
"The Blackbird by Belfast Lough" from *Kings, Lords and Commons* by
    Frank O'Connor;
"Nakatsukasa" from *Japanese Poetry*
found in *The Singing and the Gold: Poems Translated from World Literature*, selected by Elinor Parker, New York: Thomas Y. Crowell Co., 1962.

The following poems I copied into my journals over the years for my own enjoyment, not thinking that one day I would want all the publication information. I hope you can find them:
"Interlude III" by Karl Shapiro
"Something Told the Wild Geese" by Rachel Field
"Snail" by John Drinkwater
"The Hairy Dog" by Herbert Asquith
"People Buy a Lot of Things" by Annette Wynne
"Depressed By a Book of Bad Poetry, I Walk Toward an Unused
    Pasture and Invite the Insects to Join Me" by James Wright
"Wood Song" by Sara Teasdale
"A Blessing" by James Wright
"To a Squirrel at Kyle-Na-No" by W.B. Yeats

APPENDIX B

❧

Animal Pictures for Meditation

"All life is one and even the humblest forms enshrine divinity."
—Anonymous

*I*N THIS CHAPTER I would just like to introduce you to some sweet friends of mine and allow them to be appreciated. This book is about such as these little ones, and so it is only right they have a part in it. Some of these little friends I see very frequently and others not as often—but all are loving, pleasant, cheerful, and enthusiastic, and I am honored to be considered their friend. Five in this chapter are my "Grandcats" and four are my "Grandoggers." I have, too, a dear "Grandbunny" and "Grandpig" here in New Hampshire. On pages elsewhere in this book there are also pictures of Katie, Molly, and Stuffy—my "Grandoggers" who are in Heaven now—and Sweetpea, a "Grandcat." I also had a "Grandfrog," a Lake Balch frog who resided with my three grandsons for one year in Pennsylvania and is now deceased.

May these loving creatures make you smile as they peer out at you and may they touch each heart. They were very excited about having their pictures included in this book—so please enjoy their presence here.

Angel and Friday (Hudson)

Daisy (Hudson)

Tess (Kolb)

Gus (Egan)

Buddy (Egan)

Frisco (Van Dorick)

Ruthie (Drakely)

Critter (Drakely)

Fanny Mae (Drakely)

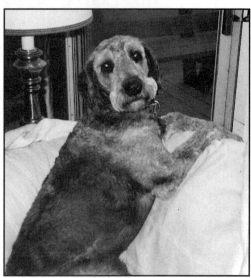

Isabel (Drakely)

❧

Passages to Ponder on Our Relationships with Animals

"Example is not the main thing in influencing others. It is the only thing."
—Albert Schweitzer

"Until we stop harming all living beings, we are still savages."
—Thomas Edison

*J*UST AS I HAVE COLLECTED POEMS through the years, much more so I have collected quotations and meaningful passages from books. These are continually recorded, and I have filled many journals so that I might go to these volumes when I need them or just merely want to browse in them to be inspired and uplifted by what is written. As years pass it would be impossible to find the quotations in each individual book that I had originally read them in, so I am thankful to have written them down in these separate journals. About three years ago I learned through my reading that I had been keeping "Commonplace Books," and that many people through the ages have done this also, writers in particular. It was interesting to learn such a collection had a name and that I was in the fine company of others who had done it or are doing it in the present. It was from this source

217

that I could share quotations that held meaning for me in my previous book, *Higher Ground*.

Throughout this book have been quotes by many individuals concerning animals and their place on this earth, their plight and suffering, and their rights. These words were penned by people of every culture and by people from other countries as well as from the United States. Now in this chapter I have included quotations by Christians exclusively, but again, not only from our own country. Again I say, these were not in abundance, as were the remarks by people of other religions or beliefs. Since Christians do speak out about their faith to others and do witness about Jesus in their lives, it cannot be then that the absence of powerful quotations regarding animals and all God's creatures is due to reserve. Yes, there are many wonderful statements, but surely not enough in comparison to all the others made by non-Christians. Though you may feel there are many in this section, the ones included took effort to find. Also, I could not find any by well-known leaders of today. Perhaps the only one you will recognize is by former President Ronald Reagan, and this is only on one area of the entire issue of animal rights. There are none who could be classified as nationally or internationally recognizable religious leaders of reputation, though I personally know two Methodist pastors and two Catholic priests in Jenkintown, Pennsylvania, and a Catholic priest in Sanbornville, New Hampshire, and my close friend Ginny, a Presbyterian Pastor in New Jersey (mentioned earlier in this book), who deeply care about the animals. Other Christian pastors are also mentioned in this book—such as the ones in the chapter, "Praying for Animals," who hold services for and are in service to them in daily life. I personally feel that we should have leaders of the clergy and in the government who speak out on behalf of God's creatures and their sufferings. So many Christians work quietly on their own or in the individual shelters or animal rights groups, and they need the voices of ones that are in higher positions to make known that there are Christians who deeply care and will not let these atrocities continue. There may be statements included in this book elsewhere that were made by Christians without my knowing they were Christians. If this be so, then please forgive me for not having known.

I do hope the quotations that are here will inspire you, that you will return to them to ponder and to pray over them, and that they will somehow guide you in your own personal way to be motivated to help the dear creatures God placed in our care on this earth. Perhaps one or two, more than the others, will strike your hearts; you could make them yours and ask God's direction concerning them.

Until you are ready to do more, I ask only that you will begin to pray for His creatures if this has not been your practice. *"More things are wrought by prayer than this world dreams of."* (Tennyson)

To recognize animal rights is a spiritual experience and a spiritual struggle. One homely example may suffice. The university where I work is situated amid acres of eighteenth-century parkland. Wildlife abounds. From my study window I observe families of wild rabbits. Looking up from my word processor from time to time, I gaze in wonder, awe and astonishment at these beautiful creatures. I sometimes say half-jokingly, "It is worth coming to the university for the rabbits." Occasionally I invite visitors to observe them. Some pause in conversation and say something like, "Oh yes," as though I had pointed out the dust on my bookshelves or the color of my carpet. What they see is not rabbits. Perhaps they see machines on four legs, "pests" that should be controlled, perhaps just other "things." It is difficult to believe that such spiritual blindness and impoverishment is the best that the superior species can manage.

—ANDREW LINZEY, Director of studies at the Center for the
Study of Theology at the University of Essex in England,
from an article, "The Theological Basis of Animal Rights,"
which appeared in *The Christian Century*

A man is truly ethical only when he obeys the compulsion to help all life which he is able to assist, and shrinks from injuring anything that lives.

—ALBERT SCHWEITZER, *The Philosophy of Civilization*

Not to hurt our humble brethren is our first duty to them, but to stop there is not enough. We have a higher mission—to be of service to them wherever they require it.

—ST. FRANCIS OF ASSISI (1181-1220), quoted in *The Life* by
Saint Bonaventure

Christ the Lord said that His Father is so concerned with birds and animals that not a sparrow falls from the sky without His notice, . . . and that foxes have dens to call home. Should we His followers be less concerned for these special products of His Creating Hand?

—REV. JOHN J. CONAHAN, Pastor, Immaculate Conception BVM Church, Jenkintown, Pennsylvania

To derive pleasure in being cruel is a very debasing matter. It shows a person to be unmindful of the sanctity of life and the meaning of life. There is something very foul and evil in the lives of men and women who delight in destroying helpless life, especially in what is known as "blood sports."

—REV. F. C. BAKER (1889-1961), quoted in "The Clergy Speak for Animals" (from *The Extended Circle*)

For fidelity, devotion, love, many a two-legged animal is below the dog and the horse. Happy would it be for thousands of people if they could stand at last before the Judgment Seat and say, "I have loved as truly and I have lived as decently as my dog." And yet we call them "only brutes."

—HENRY WARD BEECHER (1813-1887), quoted in "The Clergy Speak for Animals" (from *The Extended Circle*)

The Saints are exceedingly loving and gentle to mankind, and even to brute beasts. Surely we ought to show them (animals) great kindness and gentleness for many reasons, but, above all, because they are of the same origin as ourselves.

—ST. JOHN CHRYSOSTOM (c. 347-407), "Homilies"

Nowhere is this indifference (to animal cruelty and exploitation) in the name of fashion more evident than in the case of fur products. Fur-bearing animals trapped in the wild inevitably suffer slow agonizing deaths. Fur farms severely limit natural movement, grooming and social behavior patterns.

When we purchase the products of commercial furriers we support massive animal pain and death.

—THE WORLD COUNCIL OF CHURCHES

❧

Mans' presumption of himself as the dominant species of this world is true only in proportion to his ability to respect other species and the environment.

—ROBERT A. KOLB JR.

❧

It is no wonder that intimate acquaintance with these specimens* of the kind has taught me to hold the sportsman's amusement in abhorrence, he little knows what amiable creatures he persecutes, of what gratitude they are capable, how cheerful they are in their spirits, what enjoyment they have of life, and that, impressed as they seem with a peculiar dread of man, it is only because man gives them a peculiar cause for it.

—WILLIAM COWPER (1731-1800), published in the
Gentleman's Magazine, May 28, 1784
*from Cowper's account of his tame hares

❧

Let the law of kindness show no limits. Show a loving consideration for all God's Creatures.

—RELIGIOUS SOCIETY OF FRIENDS (Quakers)

❧

Nothing living should ever be treated with contempt. Whatever it is that lives, a man, a tree, or a bird, should be touched gently, because the time is short. . . . Civilization is another word for respect for life.

—ELIZABETH GOUDGE (1900-1984), "The Joy of the Snow"

❧

Brute beast having brains, instincts and the ability to be taught do have rights. They live on this earth with us. We have duties to humans who inhabit *the earth and breathe the air. Brute beasts are breathing that same air and living with us on that same planet. Of course we have duties to them because we certainly cannot ignore the fact they are here.*

—JANNA R. KOLB VANDORICK(daughter of the author), from a term paper on "Animal Rights" at West Chester University

❦

I hope to make people realize how totally helpless animals are, how dependent on us, trusting as a child must that we will be kind and take care of their needs. They are an obligation put on us, a responsibility we have no right to neglect, nor to violate by cruelty.

—JAMES HERRIOT (1916-), in a television interview

❦

. . . and we have so far improved upon the custom of Adam and Eve, that we generally furnish forth our feasts with a portion of some delicate calf or lamb, whose unspotted innocence entitles them to the happiness of becoming our sustenance.

—NATHANIAL HAWTHORNE (1804-1864), *The American Notebooks*

❦

A man speaks loudest of his spirituality when he silently holds and comforts an animal.

—JANICE GRAY KOLB

❦

And if thy heart be straight with God, then every creature shall be to thee a mirror of life and a book of holy doctrine, for there is no creature so little or so vile, but that sheweth and representeth the goodness of God.

—THOMAS A KEMPIS (1379-1471), *The Imitation of Christ*

He was not only, I soon discovered, a water drinker but a strict vegetarian, to which, perhaps, he owed a great deal of the almost preternatural clearness, volubility, and sensitiveness of mind.

—CHARLES KINGSLEY (1819-1875)

If people don't improve their attitude toward animals, the streets of heaven will be peopled with animals—not people.

—ROBERT A. KOLB, JR.

I despise and abhor the pleas on behalf of that infamous practice, vivisection. . . . I would rather submit to the worst of deaths, so far as pain goes, than have a single dog or cat tortured on the pretense of sparing me a twinge or two.

—ROBERT BROWNING (1812-1899), from a letter

I care not much for a man's religion whose dog and cat are not the better for it.

—ABRAHAM LINCOLN

Love of animals is a universal impulse, a common ground on which all of us may meet. By loving and understanding animals, perhaps we humans shall come to understand each other.

—DR. LOUIS J. CAMUTI (1898-1981), "All My Patients are Under the Bed"

Never believe that animals suffer less than humans. Pain is the same for them that it is for us. Even worse, because they cannot help themselves.

—DR. LOUIS J. CAMUTI (1898-1981), "Park Avenue Yet"

I was early convinced that true religion consisted in an inward life wherein the heart doth love and reverence God the Creator and learn to exercise true justice and goodness not only toward men but also toward the brute creation. . . . To say we love God as unseen, and at the same time exercise cruelty toward the least creature moving by His life or by life derived from Him, was a contradiction in itself.

—JOHN WOOLMAN (1720-1772), Quaker

✤

It is difficult to entertain a warm feeling for a medical man who can strap an unanesthetized dog on a table, cut its vocal cords and spend an interesting day—or week—slowly eviscerating or dismembering it. The researchers do not deny this themselves. They claim that despite the wholesale bloody experimentation on animals, the only real proof of the drugs found by the chemists or the operating techniques suggested by the experimentation on animals, must be, in the end, verified by trying them on human subjects.

—CLARE BOOTHE LUCE (1903-1987), address to U.S. Congress

✤

It is probable that man is perceived by God to achieve his greatest stature when he humbles himself to help an animal.

—ROBERT A. KOLB, JR.

✤

In the thirty-six years I have been a Catholic I have never heard, either in England or in France, a single sentence from the pulpit against cruelty to animals. Why not? Will not the fox hunter and the cat pot-shotter stand less chance on the Day of Judgment than the legendary lecher who is supposed to steam with lust every time he sees a buttock protruding from a Bikini? And surely it is more urgent to reprimand the cruel than the concupiscent?

—BRUCE MARSHALL, "Thoughts of my Cats" and others

I feel strongly about vivisection and although scientists endeavor to explain and justify it by the research value that its practices offer, I cannot admit these arguments as really valuable in regard to one's belief and one's faith.

—PRINCE RAINIER III of Monaco (1923-), statement to the *Anti-vivisection Magazine*

Apathy towards the animals and to any of God's creatures hardens the heart and makes one less a Christian and human being. God's will is compassion. This in turn inspires action in some form—beginning with prayer.

—JANICE GRAY KOLB

All life is precious. Let us work to inspire compassion in all human beings to care for Earth's creatures with love and kindness. God's animals need someone to speak for them. Won't you?

—ANNA C. BRIGGS, National Humane Education Society

It is a great delusion to suppose that flesh-meat of any kind is essential to health. Considerably more than three parts of the work of the world is done by men who never taste anything but vegetables, farinaceous food, and that of the simplest kind. There are far more strength-producing properties in whole wheat flour, peas, beans, lentils, oatmeal, roots, and other vegetables of the same class, than there are in beef or mutton, poultry or fish, or animal food of any description whatever.

—ORDER AND REGULATIONS OF THE OFFICERS OF THE SALVATION ARMY

Since I've given up my obsession with man's superiority over animals—I've become a better man.

—ROBERT A. KOLB, JR.

Until he extends the circle of his compassion to all living things, man will not himself find peace.

—ALBERT SCHWEITZER

🐾

My own species, unfortunately, is the greatest predator on the planet. We have the distinction of killing our own kind as well as other living creatures. But mankind is relatively new and may develop beyond this in time. . . . When people reach out to relate to animals, life is richer for both. . . . Shooting or trapping may give a momentary sense of triumph—man the powerful. But the limp body is only another victim; no more experience can come of it. Life has more to give than death.

—GLADYS TABOR (1899-), author

🐾

Let every creature have your love. Love, with its fruits of meekness, patience, and humility, is all that we can wish for ourselves, and our fellow creatures: for this is to live in God, united to Him, both for time and eternity.

—WILLIAM LAW (1686-1761), "A Serious Call to a Devout and Holy Life"

🐾

Gandhi said, "I do feel that spiritual progress does demand at some state that we should cease to kill off our fellow creatures for the satisfaction of our bodily wants." Brute beasts have the right to live life in their natural habitats to the fullest, just as humans do.

—JANNA R. KOLB VANDORICK

🐾

Lack of understanding is often stated and chosen so one does not have to become involved.

—JANICE GRAY KOLB

There is no life so meager that the greatest and wisest of us can afford to despise it. We cannot know at all what sudden moment it may flash forth with the life of God.

—PHILLIPS BROOKS (1835-1893), Sermons

Are we to pity only creatures whose appearance pleases us? It is not because they are small or ugly that mice and rats don't suffer when they are torn apart.

—BRUCE MARSHALL, from "Thoughts of My Cats"

I only wish more animals were free to share their sweet companionship in good health and good spirits, as God so clearly intended them to do.

—ANNA C. BRIGGS, National Humane Education Society

The world can only approach true peace when not only the lamb lies down with the lion, but when they both can lie down with man.

—ROBERT A. KOLB, JR.

As long as I can remember, I have suffered because of the great misery I see in the world. I never really knew the artless youthful joy of living, and I believe that many children feel this way, even when outwardly they seem to be wholly happy and without a single care. I used to suffer particularly because the poor animals must endure so much pain and want. The sight of an old, limping horse being dragged along by one man while another man struck him with a stick—he was being driven to the Colmar slaughterhouse—tortured me for weeks.

—ALBERT SCHWEITZER

I write in sorrow (on vivisection): as far as I can tell, no voice has been heard from the church about this evil. The matter is forgotten for another year. It should not be. It is one of the most appalling blots on our plentifully blotted civilization.

          —REV. GEOFFREY MATHER (1910-), *Church Times*, October
            20, 1972

In Matthew 7:12 it states, "Do unto others as you would have them do unto you." And in Isaiah 66:3 it says that "Killing a cow is the equivalent of killing a human." God breathed life into all creatures. Just because humans can speak and have a higher intellect, they feel they have the right to do as they please to other living creatures—whether it be for science, needs, convenience, or food.

          —JANNA R. KOLB VANDORICK

Haven't enough animals been drowned, shocked, burned, starved, deprived, blinded, deafened, maimed, cut, and poisoned—all in the name of science? Here at the National Humane Education Society, we believe the dark age of vivisection should be ended. And with the help of kind-hearted supporters across the country, we hope to bring about the dawning of a new age of kindness to all of God's creatures.

          —ANNA C. BRIGGS, National Humane Education Society
            (founded 1948)

We consume the carcasses of creatures of like appetites, passions and organs with our own, and fill the slaughter houses daily with screams of pain and fear.

          —ROBERT LOUIS STEVENSON (1850-1894)

Since factory farming exerts a violent and unnatural force upon the living organisms of animals and birds in order to increase production and profits. Since it involves callous and cruel exploitation of life, with implicit contempt for nature, I must join in the protest being uttered against it. It does not seem that these methods have any really justifiable purpose, except to increase the quantity of production at the expense of quality—if that can be called a justifiable purpose.

However there is only one aspect of a more general phenomenon: the increasingly destructive and irrational behaviour of technological man. Our society seems to be more and more oriented at over-production, to waste, and finally to production for destruction. Its orientation to global war is the culminating absurdity of its inner logic—or lack of logic. The mistreatment of animals in "intensive husbandry" is, then, part of this larger picture of insensitivity to genuine values and indeed to humanity and life itself—a picture which more and more comes to display the ugly lineaments of what can only be called by its right name: barbarism.

—THOMAS MERTON (1915-1968), from "Unlived Life" (*The Extended Circle*)

I felt vegetarianism to be more consistent with the Christian faith I hold, and in particular with the repudiation of violence, which for me is an integral part of the faith.

I would not pretend for a moment that Christians can be completely consistent in this imperfect world, but aesthetically as well as ethically I have felt a strong sense of satisfaction—a peace of mind, if you like—since I took this decision.

Godliness with contentment is great gain.

—REV. LORD (DONALD) SOPER (1903-), *The British Vegetarian*, March/April 1959 (quoted in *The Extended Circle*)

Twice, in the company of other boys, I went fishing with a rod! But then my horror in mistreatment of the impaled worms—and at the tearing of the mouths of the fishes when they were caught—made it impossible for me to continue. Indeed, I even found the courage to dissuade others from fishing.

—ALBERT SCHWEITZER (Kindheit)

I shudder even to think about the experiments done on animals in the name of science and progress, but I must make myself write about it, in the hopes that others will share my outrage, and that together we will be able to put an end to vivisection in all its forms.

—ANNA C. BRIGGS, National Humane Education Society

❧

It is almost a definition of a gentleman to say he is one who never inflicts pain.

—CARDINAL NEWMAN

❧

Since "Asta" (my Wire-Haired Fox Terrier) made her entry into my life this past October—my loneliness has been taken away. In sharing her with others they come to know and love her too. Because of her I have new responsibilities and she places a trust in me to care for her that is the same as the trust of a child. Those who love animals could never hurt them! Above all, Asta is a channel of God's Love to me and through her I experience this love in a special way. Asta is "Wonder Dog," "Faithful Companion," and "Parish Pooch," and from the Rectory window she enjoys seeing the parishioners go to and from church—as they enjoy seeing her. ASTA IS JOY!

—REV. EDMUND A. BABICZ, Pastor, St. Anthony of Padua Parish, Sanbornville, New Hampshire

❧

Recollect that the Almighty who gave the dog to be the companion of our pleasures and our toils, hath invested him with a nature noble and incapable of deceit.

—SIR WALTER SCOTT

❧

Wild animals never kill for sport. Man is the only one to whom the torture and death of his fellow creatures is amusing in itself.

—JAMES ANTHONY FROUDE

Dumb animals? Are you kidding!? Animals may not speak English but they have their own ways of communicating. They are vocal—over 60 different "meows" have been observed among domestic cats. Animals also use body language effectively among their own species and with us if we are caring and observant. Watch ears, eyes, tails, heads and feet. Any part of an animal's body can express a feeling or a request. We and our pets or work animals will have a richer more satisfying partnership if we humans will pay attention to what our animals are saying.

—MARILY S. RICHARDS

Christians may say they dislike animals—but it is through praying for those we dislike that God changes our hearts.

—JANICE GRAY KOLB

For Mr. Briggs, being a vegetarian followed out of his commitment to animals. He told how cattle and sheep on trains and in slaughterhouses suffered miserably. From that day on (1925), I have never eaten flesh, and I have never missed it. Nor did my children eat meat or fish. Yet, contrary to popular belief, we were all healthy, able to out-work many of our meat-eating counterparts.

—ANNA C. BRIGGS, National Humane Education Society

Now what is it moves our very heart, and sickens us so much as the cruelty shown to poor brutes? I suppose this: first, that they have done us no harm; next, that they have no power whatever of resistance; it is the cowardice and tyranny of which they are victims which make their suffering so especially touching. . . . There is something so very dreadful, so Satanic in tormenting those who have never harmed us, and who cannot defend themselves, who are utterly in our power.

—CARDINAL NEWMAN (1801-1890), Parochial and Plain Sermons

Without perfect sympathy with the animals around them, no gentleman's education, no Christian education, could be of any possible use.

> —JOHN RUSKIN (1819-1900), speech to the Society of Prevention of Cruelty to Animals

Somewhere in my Christian training I learned a basic respect for animals as an important part of God's Creation. Today I'm concerned about the "Canary Effect."* So many animal species are now extinct—we need a reconciliation between humankind, animals, and the environment, or else we will lose the crucial balance that will make life possible.

> —REV. DONALD E. RICHARDS, Pastor, Jenkintown United Methodist Church, Jenkintown, Pennsylvania
> *Refers to the past practice of taking caged canaries into the mines to give warning, by their deaths, when the air supply became contaminated and was approaching an unsafe level for humans.

We need to maintain the value, the preciousness of the human by affirming the preciousness of the non-human also—of all that is. For our concept of God forbids the idea of a cheap creation, of a throw-away universe in which everything is expendable save human existence.

> —ANGLICAN ARCHBISHOP ROBERT RUNCIE, stated in 1988

Animals, as part of God's Creation, have rights which must be respected. It behooves us always to be sensitive to their needs and to the reality of their pain.

> —ANGLICAN ARCHBISHOP DONALD COOGAN, stated in 1877

There's an emotional issue that has the potential to harm Japan greatly—the issue of the environment. There is growing news coverage of Japan's role in the loss of endangered species, in the practices of drift-net fishing and tropical logging. No country is without blame when it comes to the environment, but

Japan will come under increasing pressure, perhaps even the boycott of Japanese products.

> —FORMER PRESIDENT RONALD REAGAN in a 1989 speech to Japanese leaders

🐾

Whether or not we find it practicable and desirable, the diet assigned to men and beasts by God the Creator is vegetarian.

> —KARL BARTH (Church Dogmatics)

🐾

The diminution of experimentation on animals, which has progressively been made ever less necessary, corresponds to the plan and well-being of all creation.

> —POPE JOHN PAUL II, in *The National Catholic Reporter*, 1982

🐾

According to the theological doctrine of animal rights, then, humans are to be the servant species: the species given power, opportunity and privilege to give themselves, nay sacrifice themselves, for the weaker, suffering creatures. I for one, have never claimed any strict moral equality between humans and animals. . . . In my view, what we owe animals is more than equal consideration, equal treatment or equal concern. The weak, the powerless, the disadvantaged, the oppressed should not have equal moral priority but greater moral priority. When we minister to the least of all we minister to Christ himself. To follow Jesus is to accept axiomatically that the weak have moral priority. Our special value as a species consists in being of special value for others.

> —Andrew Linzey, "The Theological Basis of Animal Rights" from *The Christian Century*

🐾

Amen
May these quotations in some way aid
in overcoming the Ostrich Syndrome

MY SELLA*

The shadow of my soul—my heart
Is a soft and furry counterpart
Of all I am and feel and think—
And a most mysterious link
With God. A consecrated connection
Sent by Him, a perfection
Of love and joy, one who is always there
Waiting to follow. Such a pair
My Sella and I—for we
Are bonded spiritually—
One in Him—God drew no line.
My Sella, My Shadow—is divine—
And overshadows me in comprehending
The unseen realm. In gratitude for sending
This gift of playfulness, peace and protection—
I pause daily in awe and reflection
Upon this inseparable companion—this life force—
And I humbly thank Him—our Source.

—JGK
April 10, 1996
New Hampshire

Dedicated to my Rochester, my Sella
with love
in the estimated month of his birth

* Sella means Shadow
Taken from the poem
by that name
written by
William Cullen Bryant

INEXPRESSIBLE

Words that cannot form expression—
Are heart words that refuse confession.
Words that have no earthly speech
From soul to world; invisible breech!
And yet we oft' times can convey
These feelings that just disobey—
Our strivings to make them perform
Deliver warm—behave—conform.

Our actions speak our inner thought—
Though often they too fall to naught.
Our soul then must reflect through eyes—
Reveal through windows love and sighs.
God gave this way to manifest—
All that is best—all that is blest.

And so this day and in this way—
May my soul's windows show—I pray,
My gratitude that has no end—
For priceless gift of eternal friend—
Put in my life—(such sweet intrusion!)
For melded hearts in instant fusion.

O dear faithful companion—all love and purrs—
At your ever constant presence—my soul stirs.

Thank you, Lord—for the gift of Rochester.

—Janice Gray Kolb
Dedicated to
Rochester Harry Whittier Kolb
on the 5th anniversary of his entering our lives.
June 23, 1991

And thank you, Lord—that through and because of Rochester—
this book came to be.

ROCHESTER   OWNER: JANICE KOLB

Picture of Rochester as he appears in the Humane Society of America's Desk Calendar for 1996. In the accompanying letter of congratulations it stated that he was chosen from over 20,000 entries. I have always had Thanksgiving in my heart for him in my life—so I was deeply moved to learn his picture appears on Thanksgiving Day—November 28, 1996. I had wished to honor him and entered his photo in the contest. —JGK

ALL GOD'S CREATURES
by
Robert A. Kolb Jr.

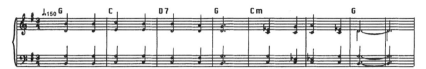

(1) All God's creatures have some rights—Man and Beast and Fowl.
(2) If we call Him Father God—then it must be true.
(3) How can we without a thought—say the "Golden Rule"
(4) All God's Creatures have more rights—than just live and die.
(5) Man's dominion doesn't mean—he must subjugate.

(1) Every little sparrow—each fox and every cow.
(2) That we're surely brothers—to things He Fathered too.
(3) Then abuse God's creatures—willfully be so cruel.
(4) We are often heartless—don't even really try.
(5) All God's precious creatures—should man control their fate?

(1) All are part of His Great Plan—for he loves us all.
(2) For He blew the breath of life—into every breast.
(3) Oft' compassion is ignored—we should turn in shame.
(4) We sit back and then pretend—that we do not see.
(5) There's responsibility—not just selfish gain.

(1) If we love Him then we must love—creatures Great and Small.
(2) Placed a spirit deep down inside—and all creatures blessed.
(3) From the least—the last—and the lost—from the sick and lame.
(4) God's dear face and hear His strong voice—"Let my creatures free!."
(5) And compassion for all of life—and all creatures pain.

Declaration of The Rights of Animals

Whereas it is self-evident

That we share the earth with other creatures, great and small,
That many of these animals experience pleasure and pain,
That these animals deserve our just treatment and
That these animals are unable to speak for themselves,

We do therefore declare that these animals

Have the right to live free from human exploitation, whether in the name of science or sport, exhibition or service, food or fashion;
Have the right to live in harmony with their nature rather than according to human desires;
Have the right to live on a healthy planet.

This declaration on animal rights was proclaimed and adopted by the 30,000 participants in the March for the Animals in Washington, DC on June 10, 1990.

—from *The Animal Rights Handbook: Everyday Ways To Save Animal Lives)*

Advertisement for Wildlife Siren

This product can be purchased to put on the outside of your car. Once attached in an inconspicuous place it is activated by the passage of air through it and will help save the lives of all creatures and wildlife.

Animal Saver System©

Airflow Produces Ultrasonic Sound.
(Animals in side car are not affected)
Saves
Deer • Dogs • Cats • Farm Animals and Other Wild Life

Reference Books for Further Reading

Abehsera, Michel. *Zen Macrobiotic Cooking* (Oriental and Traditional Recipes). New York: Avon Books, 1970.

The Animal Rights Handbook: Every Day Ways to Save Animal Lives. Venice, CA: Living Planet Press, 1990

Armory, Cleveland. *The Cat Who Came for Christmas.* Boston, Toronto, London: Little, Brown & Co., 1987.

Armory, Cleveland. *The Cat and the Curmudgeon.* Boston, Toronto, London: Little, Brown & Co., 1990.

Boone, J. Allen. *Kinship With All Life.* New York: Harper & Row, 1954, 1976.

Briggs, Anna C. *For the Love of Animals.* Potomac Publishing Co., 1990. (The story of the National Humane Education Society.)

Bustad, D.V.M., Ph.D., Leo K. *Compassion: Our Last Great Hope.* Selected speeches. Renton, WA: The Delta Society, 1990.

Camuti, Dr. Louis J. with Frankel, Marilyn & Haskel. *All My Patients Are Under the Bed.* New York: Simon & Schuster, 1980. (Memoirs of a cat doctor.)

Caras, Roger A. *A Cat Is Watching.* New York: Simon & Schuster, 1989. (A look at the way cats see us.)

Caras, Roger A. *The Cats of Thistle Hill—A Mostly Peaceable Kingdom.* New York: Simon & Schuster, 1994.

Diamond, Marilyn. *The American Vegetarian Cookbook.* New York: Warner Books, 1990.

Fox, Dr. Michael W. & Weintraub, Pamela. *You Can Save the Animals: 50 Things to Do Right Now.* New York: St. Martin's Press, 1991.

Frazier, Anita with Eckroate, Norma. *The Natural Cat: A Holistic Guide for Finicky Owners, Revised Edition.* New York: Dutton, 1981, 1983, 1991.

Gallico, Paul W. (Transl. from the Feline & Ed.) *The Silent Miaow.* New York: Crown Publishers, 1985.

George, Jean Craighead. *How to Talk to Your Cat.* New York: Warner Books, 1985. (Offers insight into animal communication. Also *How to Talk to Your Dog.*)

Herriot, James. *All Things Wise and Wonderful.* New York: St. Martins Press, 1977. (Also *All Things Bright and Beautiful*, *All Creatures Great and Small*, and other books.)

Jenkins, Peter. *Close Friends.* New York: William Morrow and Co., 1985. (Warm, loving memories of his most remarkable pets and companions. Author of best seller, *Walk Across America*, and others.)

Joy, Charles R. (Transl. & Ed.). *The Animal World of Albert Schweitzer: Jungle Insights into Reverence for Life.* Boston: Beacon Press, 1950, 1959.

Koller, Alice. *The Stations of Solitude.* New York: William Morrow and Co., 1990.

Kosins, Martin Scot. *Maya's First Rose (A Memoir of Undying Devotion for Anyone Who Has Ever Lost a Pet).* New York: Berkley Publishing, 1992, 1994, 1996.

Kowalski, Gary. *The Souls of Animals.* Walpole, NH: Stillpoint Publishing, 1991.

Marshall, Bruce. *Thoughts of My Cats.* Boston: Houghton Mifflin, 1954.

Masson, Jeffrey Moussaieff & McCarthy, Susan. *When Elephants Weep: The Emotional Lives of Animals.* New York: Delacorte Press, 1995.

Morris, Desmond (author of *Catwatching, Dogwatching, Horsewatching, Catlore,* and others). *The Animal Contract.* London: Virgin Books, 1990.

Newkirk, Ingrid (National Director, People for the Ethical Treatment of Animals [PETA]). *Save the Animals: 101 Easy Things You Can Do*. New York: Warner Books, 1990.

Newkirk, Ingrid. *Kids Can Save the Animals! 101 Easy Things You Can Do*. New York: Warner Books, 1991.

Sattilaro, Dr. Anthony. *Recalled by Life*. Boston: Houghton Mifflin, 1982.

Sequoia, Anna. *67 Ways to Save the Animals*. New York: HarperCollins, 1990.

Singer, Peter. *Animal Liberation*. New York: New York Review of Books, 1975, 1990. (Considered the "Bible" of the Animal Rights Movement.)

Singer, Peter (Ed.). *In Defense of Animals*. New York: Harper & Row, 1985.

Townsend, Irving (Collector). *Separate Lifetimes*. Exeter, NH: J.N. Townsend Pub., 1986, 1990.

Wynne-Tyson, Jon (Ed.). *The Extended Circle: A Commonplace Book of Animal Rights*. New York: Paragon House, 1985, 1989.

About the Author

Janice Kolb along with her husband Bob are the parents of six grown children and have thirteen grandchildren. Their life has revolved around raising a loving family with religious values. In addition to raising their family, Janice developed a letter writing and audio tape ministry in order to encourage and spiritually support those who need it all over the United States.

Other inspirational works by Janice Kolb include: *Higher Ground*, *The Pine Cone Journal*, and *Silent Violence*. In a cooperative effort, Janice wrote the book *Whispered Notes* with her husband Bob.

Bob Kolb
helped me with this book so much and
has typed this and everything else I have written.
I could not have done it without him,
as the manuscript was all written in longhand.